NAVIGATING THROUGH FEAR

Learn to Live an Enriched Life Using
Spirit's Compass to Guide You

Susan Elaine Stewart

Workbook Sections Follow Each Chapter

With Practical Suggestions for

Diminishing Fear and Improving Risk-Taking Skills

Peak View Publications

Published by Peak View Publications / peakviewpublications.com

Copyright © 2006 by Susan E. Stewart

Cover photographs, "Sunrise on the Mediterranean" and "Rainbow

Over Montbrun, France," copyright ©2006 by Susan E. Stewart.

Contact author at: SusanStewart@peakviewpublications.com

I would like to gratefully acknowledge all the writers I have quoted for all

of their wisdom, inspiration and encouragement. If there have been errors

in the quotes or if I have failed to appropriately request permission to

reprint these quotes, I apologize, and a correction will be made in

subsequent editions.

"Rivers Hardly Ever" by James Dillet Freeman published with

permission of Unity, www.unityonline.org

ISBN # 978-1-4303-0871-3

*For their wonderful gift of love that
taught me I have all I need within me to be
wise, loving and extraordinary,
I dedicate this book to my mother,
Lois Annette Daish Stewart House, and to
my grandmother, Hazel McGregor Daish*

Table of Contents

Chapter 1   Finding Your Way / 1

Chapter 2   The Path of Most Resistance / 7

Chapter 3   Are You Ripe? / 16

Chapter 4   Flying by the Seat of Your Pants /23

Chapter 5   Courage Expands With Use / 31

Chapter 6   When Your Boat Needs Rocking / 39

Chapter 7   When Push Needs a Little Shove / 45

Chapter 8   Shoulda, Coulda, Woulda / 51

Chapter 9   Mortality Therapy Enlivens / 61

Chapter 10   A Flyspeck Won't Be Noticed / 69

Chapter 11   Delectable Burnt Marshmallows / 77

Chapter 12   Going With the Flow / 87

Chapter 13 Flowing With the Go / 97

Chapter 14 Unfolding Like an Exquisite Flower/ 106

Chapter 15 When the Flower Opens the Bees
           Will Come /114

Chapter 16 Following Spirit's Compass / 121

Chapter 17 Looking Beyond Appearances /129

Chapter 18 All People Smile in the Same
           Language / 138

Chapter 19 Angels Disguised As Friends / 146

Chapter 20 Giving the Gift of Receiving / 153

Chapter 21 Surrender to Live / 160

Chapter 22 Don't Just Do Something, Sit There / 168

Suggested Readings from the Author / 178

About the Author / 180

Acknowledgments

Everyone deserves to have "leg-up" people in their life who boost them up when they need a lift. I acknowledge with joy and pleasure my friends and family who have been just such people as I forged through the creation of this book. I am especially grateful to my children, Jocelyn and Brandon, for their love, support and encouragement of my never-ending adventures. They both truly grasp living the courageous life that I teach in this book. To Kurtis Kelly, I give heartfelt thanks. As an editor, he not only guided and advised me through the writing process, but he has also supported me for years, with fabulous humor, in moving ahead with my projects. I am very appreciative to two other editors, Ethan Stemm and Diane Patterson, who both stepped in and encouraged me to fine-tune my piece even more. All three of these people contributed immensely to this book, lovingly challenging me to challenge myself. I am very grateful to my friend, Amanda Harrison, who never quit believing in my vision, and by giving me opportunities to be published, sparked my enthusiasm for writing. I also want to thank Rick Patterson and Lauren Smart for their technical assistance in transforming this baby from thought to paper, but more importantly for their encouragement and friendship. And thanks to another talented artist and friend, Deb Wolf, who designed my publishing logo. I am fortunate to have many other supportive friends and family whose love and laughter continually sustain me, assisting me to move in the direction of my dreams. My appreciation for you never ends. And lastly, but certainly not least, I want to thank all of my clients along the way who dared to share their struggles and triumphs with me. Your honesty, trust in me and courage to change is an incredible gift that has given me reason to believe in the magnificence of the human spirit.

Suggestions to My Readers

I have written this book to share with you my readers what I have learned about fear and risk-taking from my many clients over the past 24 years. I also share from my own life experiences, specifically from a solo backpacking pilgrimage I made through Europe as a 50 year-old.

I have set up this book to take you along with me as I travel through Europe, but more importantly to teach what I know about living a full, rich life. The greatest deterrent to a good life is fear, as I believe fear robs all of us of joy and peace. I have carefully selected many quotations from wise and wonderful people that encourage us to get past our fears so that we may taste our life experiences to the utmost. I propose that you select your favorite few quotes and place them where you can view them daily.

Following each chapter, there is a workbook section with questions for you to consider and space for you to write as you gain insight into yourself. I suggest you contemplate each question carefully, be as honest with yourself as possible, and be courageous enough to examine your fears and their sources. As you face your fears, looking them straight in the eye, you'll be pleasantly surprised how amazingly they dissolve.

The purpose of life is to live it,
to taste experience to the utmost,
to reach out eagerly and without
fear for newer and richer experience.

----- *Eleanor Roosevelt*

CHAPTER ONE

FINDING YOUR WAY

*(Explorers) are persons in motion, passing
through territories not their own seeking...
completion or clarity, a goal to which only
spirit's compass points the way.*

----- *H. Richard Niebuhr*

Part way up the beautiful path behind the magnificent Basilica at Lourdes, France, I stood looking down upon the gentle river flowing past the cave where St. Bernadette saw visions of the Virgin Mary. The visions instructed her that this was a holy place and that it would become a place of healing for millions of people. There along the tree-lined path is an Italian statue with an inscription, which translated into French says,

"Retrouver ta Foi c'est plus que
retrouver la vue."

Translated into English: "It is more to rediscover your faith, than to rediscover the view." The specific definition of retrouver is "to find one's way again, to rediscover, to regain one's strength, to

1

find again." What a great gift to me just four days before the end of my journey!

All of a sudden I *knew* why I had pushed through my fears to leave familiar surroundings and launch into the unknown. My entire being had found the decision to take a journey of self exploration enormously difficult. My mind attempted to dissuade me, my logic cried out in fear, as I quit my job, left my home and belongings with a complete stranger and sold my car just to finance this journey. I needed to find the self of me that had gotten lost, explore my life's purpose and reignite my passion for living. I had abandoned what seemed to be safe and soothing to enter into an expansion of self that felt disturbingly uncomfortable.

> *We don't receive wisdom; we must*
> *discover it for ourselves after a journey*
> *that no one can take for us or spare* us.
>
> ----- *Marcel Proust*

Now, standing above hundreds of bright, burning candles near St. Bernadette's cave, *I felt the simple peace of knowing*. At last I understood my inner nudge to take the risks needed to complete a solo journey throughout Europe.

All my challenging efforts to expand my comfort zone and walk through my fears had been very well rewarded. I finally recognized the incredible wisdom and power I had attained. Back home amidst the routine of daily living, I had gotten lost in deep ruts of unfulfillment. Some inner knowing had urged me to rediscover myself, to regain my strength, to find my way again. I found answers to questions I had been asking myself repeatedly throughout the months of my journey, but indeed for much, much longer. Questions such as:

Why am I here? How can I experience peace every day despite what is going on in my outer world? How do I transform my fears into serenity?

I have spent my days stringing and unstringing my instrument while the song I came to sing remains unsung.

----- *Rabindranath Tagore*

And that rediscovery, that process, had to be accomplished by letting go of the everyday distractions I had skillfully used to keep me from knowing my true self -- preoccupations such as my children, men, my work, dirty dishes or the car insurance bill. Suddenly I knew by looking deep within myself (which is indeed a frightening assignment), that I would have to let go of the petty dramas I create daily just to distract myself from what is real and important. My risk-taking had taught me to quit turning my head, to put down my blinders and to stop ignoring those nagging urges *to be more* that had been hanging around me for years. Instead, I knew it was time to bring the fears, those self-created monsters, and place them right in front of me. I needed to look them straight in the eye. Reach out. Touch them. Prove they were only illusions.

I simply could no longer tolerate living a fear-based life.

This voice inside me that had directed me to take this journey clearly instructed it to be a vision quest. It needed to be much more than just a trip, or an attempt to physically move my body, but rather a pilgrimage that would help me discover meaning for my life through lessons I would encounter. The deepest part of my soul was hungry to learn. I wanted to become *enlightened,* to find some truth beyond my human superficial self. I wanted to **be at peace.**

One doesn't discover new lands without consenting to lose sight of the shore for a very long time.

----- *Andre Gide*

Tools for Navigating Through Your Fears

- What activities do you engage in that keep you continually "stringing and unstringing your instrument" rather than singing the song that you came here to sing? Make a list of those distractions and add to it as you remember more throughout your week.

  - watching useless TV
  - reading PEOPLE magazine & travel magazines
  - cooking

- Can you identify the "song" that you believe you are here to sing? In other words, what do you feel is your purpose? If you are struggling with that, which most humans do, perhaps you can begin to open yourself to the possibilities that may help clarify your purpose. When you examine this subject, it helps to think of defining a "Mission Statement" for your life…a proclamation in broad terms that declares what you believe your life is about.

  - To serve the Lord with gladness.
  - To encourage others.
  - Open myself to love both myself & others.

- What behavior or personality trait would you like to re-discover or find again in yourself that perhaps you have lost or set aside for some time?

- laughter
- childlike wonder
- being positive &
  uplifting

- living w/ an
  abundance of enthusiasm.

- honor my own
  sacredness

CHAPTER TWO

THE PATH OF MOST RESISTANCE

Our fears must never hold us back
from pursuing our hopes.

-----*John F. Kennedy*

This book is about fear. Its gift to you is to help you rediscover your genuine self, to regain your strength, to encourage you to live a more expansive, richer life, to help you live with complete authenticity and become all that you were created to be. I encourage you to replace anxiety, worry, cautiousness and trepidation with a delightful zest for living! Isn't it time to experience enthusiasm for your life and a joy in adventuring? Would you like to be able to taste each experience in every moment to the utmost?

The lessons in these pages are about risk-taking behaviors that pour treasures upon us that we cannot even see at the time. This is about opening the closed door, walking through fear and having the courage to "handle it," whatever *it* may be for you. It is also about you learning to honor your own Sacredness. However that looks and feels for you. It is only then that you are able to honor the Sacredness in all other beings. This brings peace...and there is no greater gift than inner peace.

As a family therapist for the past 24 years, I have learned priceless lessons from my clients, the average Joe, who may be like you. They strive to be happy, but seem unable to let go of learned behaviors that haunt them with frustration or anxiety and put happiness out of reach. It has been such a joy for me to watch people unfold, grow into *more*, become healthier, stronger and very self-confident. They have taught me how resilient the human spirit is! By replacing thoughts of worry with the ability to go with the flow, to *allow* rather than control, people feel peace instead of anxiety. They gain and use perspective to thrive. And trust that all is well, despite adversity and challenge.

I met a lot of people in Europe.
I even encountered myself.

----- *James Baldwin*

Are you willing to open your mind and heart? I am ready to share what these phenomenal people have taught me, as well as share the valuable lessons I gained from my back-packing journey through Europe as a 50 year-old. Rather than spending time, lots of money and agony analyzing the events of our childhood to hopefully figure out what makes us tick, what our life's purpose is, instead why not learn through the experiences of each other?

8

You can learn through these teachings to relax, lighten up, and be the playful, trusting, loving child you are inside. You were born not having to worry about thinking, saying or doing the right things. You simply were – you. You were beautiful then. You still are. You knew how to share your love without bias, feeling that connecting to people was as natural as a bird gliding through the air.

I believe that **fear** is the basis of why I have had a thriving family therapy practice. Feelings of inadequacy, low self-esteem, frustration and dissatisfaction are ultimately what push people through my door. But the tree from which these bothersome by-products stem is the tree of fear. If my theory is correct that fear robs us of love, specifically self-love, then it follows that fear is also the fuel that keeps the fire of low self-esteem burning. It's a blaze that travels quickly and furiously throughout our beings. It spreads through our families, communities, our nation and even the world.

The willingness to consider possibility
requires a tolerance of uncertainty.
----- *Rachel Naomi Remen, M.D.*

Without high regard for ourselves, how do we find courage to overcome stagnation, to reach out, to move upward and onward? The tree of fear becomes so massive that it blocks our path to peace and joy. As we allow this roadblock to keep us stuck in anxiety, we

9

tend to continue our unsatisfying lifestyles or relationships. In order to become all that we were created to be, to live utilizing our full potential, we must first examine the fear and ensuing sense of inadequacy that traps us.

Our answers are in our questioning. The solution is in the problem. By ignoring the fear, pretending it's not there and distracting ourselves from even acknowledging it, we are in a sense fertilizing that fear tree. We actually perpetuate it, encourage it to grow, by telling ourselves it's not there. There is only one way to diminish the power it has over us.

Face it.

There is perhaps nothing so bad
and so dangerous in life as fear.
----- Jawaharlal Nehru,
India's First Prime Minister, 1947

We must first admit we feel fear and acknowledge that it is robbing us of joy and keeping us trapped. We can't change anything until we admit its existence. If you're sick and tired of fear and anxiety controlling your life, get out the chainsaw and hack away! Use the fuel created by the power, strength and courage that are abundantly stored within you. Let's begin by trimming away old concepts to make room for new risk-taking behaviors.

As we allow fear to restrict our lives, we sadly wall ourselves off from others, from love, from life itself. For example, past hurts may create fear of more hurt, so we play it safe by closing ourselves off from the possibility of new relationships. We were born not only to live fully and free from fear, but life is actually *easier* when we follow our natural design. Our natural design is joy and ease, a knowing that all is well, despite what we conjure up in our heads.

As we resist what is our nature, *we actually create unnecessary agony for ourselves.* We hide behind our defenses and rationalizations, entering caves of darkness, and work very hard to convince ourselves in amazingly creative ways that the cave is what life is supposed to be. We remain for years in jobs that are unfulfilling as we persuade ourselves we can't move on because of security, money or "benefits." Or we fail to take enjoyable vacations because we're afraid to let go of some savings, leave the dog with a sitter or fly in a plane.

First of all, let me assert my firm belief
that the only thing we have to fear is fear
itself - nameless, unreasoning, unjustified
terror which paralyzes needed effort
to convert retreat into advance.
----- Franklin Delano Roosevelt

Meanwhile, the sun shines brightly outside, flowers abound in technicolor, and yes, a few rare and brave souls have ventured out there. They are playing, laughing and enjoying themselves, each other, and the many life-adventures offered freely for our pleasure and enjoyment. They have learned to live freely, walk over their fears on a tightrope of faith, often without so much as a safety net, viewing risk as a delightful challenge that ultimately becomes their ally. You, too, can begin to change your view of risking from enemy to friend as you read on.

In the past few years, it seems that our lives as a collective community are being controlled largely by fear. We forget that we've all been hurt, we've all experienced trauma and we've all felt out of control at times. Our wounds, memories of pain and fear of more of the same delude us into thinking that hiding will keep us nice and safe. The truth is, however, we just *think* avoidance is helping. Evading our own trepidations is actually causing just the opposite of what we want and need! Fear grows when it is ignored. As we further explore these ideas, we will examine the entire concept of control versus letting go, but a challenging idea to initially consider is:

The true irony is that the only way to feel in control is to absolutely let go of attempting to control.

The more I traveled, the more I realized that fear makes strangers of people who should be friends."

-----*Shirley MacLaine*

12

It doesn't really matter why we are so determir
our status quo (complaining all the while about our bor
that some revelations might give us insight that will help us change.
One author who has encouraged me to examine my own fear-based
"stuck-ness" is Gregg Levoy in his beautiful and thoughtful book,
Callings: Finding and Following An Authentic Life. His messages
have been an incredible inspiration to me and were a constant source
of support throughout my journey. He eloquently writes, "The desire
to protect ourselves from change probably does more harm to the
flowering of human life and spirit than almost any other choice, but it
is imperative to understand something about security: It isn't secure!
Everything about security is contrary to the central fact of existence:
Life changes. By trying to shelter ourselves from change, we isolate
ourselves from living."

The more we avoid change or cling to "security," the greater
our fears become. The more predominant our fears, the more we
avoid change. These behaviors are all connected and constantly
influencing each other. As we stay trapped tightly in our limited
caves, the dark shadows of fear grow larger and more powerful. We
stagnate rather than expand. Boredom and lack of fulfillment take
over. Before you know it, you're 80 years old and wondering why you
didn't live your life with more zeal and less fear. It's difficult to
recognize the entrapments. But, happily, not impossible.

The most common regrets people talk about on their
deathbeds are the things they did not do in life, not what they did.
And our fears -- of failure, of looking like a fool, of wondering what

others will think if we goof -- can hold us in our self-imposed prison, just as surely as chains and shackles can restrain our bodies. The poetic and wise lyrics of the Eagles song "Already Gone" (J. Tempchin and R. Stradlund) speak of this. "So often times it happens that we live our lives in chains, and we never even know we have the key."

I hear you asking, "Just where do I find this key?" The choice to either reach out to life, sometimes risking failure, or hiding safe within your cave, is yours to make. I'm confident that you *can* find the key to unlock your freedom and this book is dedicated to helping you face your fears. Perhaps you can begin by looking for the key within your heart.

Not life, but good life, is to be chiefly valued.

----- *Socrates*

Tools for Navigating Through Your Fears

— Mom struggling on her own

- Name all your recurring fears. Yes, grab some extra paper and write them down and look at them in black and white. Just start spieling them out of your heart and head as fast as you can write them down. Don't forget to list them all…even those that sound silly and seem ridiculous! Hold onto the list

— being used, manipulated, controlled

being / alone by Lyon

losing

14 — being physically sexually harmed by Victor

and add to it as you remember more. Continue to sa.
you will need it later.

- What specific activities are you avoiding because of any of
  these fears? (i.e. risking getting involved in a love
  relationship because of past heartaches and the fear of more
  pain)

  - staying married to Vicky

  - finding fault w/men

  to avoid emotional

  intimacy

- To begin finding the key that unlocks your self-imposed
  chains, ask yourself honestly: "What is my gut reaction, my
  emotional response, when I write about these fears?" Then
  ask yourself if you enjoy your responses; if not, how
  determined are you to move beyond them?

CHAPTER THREE

ARE YOU RIPE?

If you're getting directions, 'Move on with your life, let go of something,' then do it. Have the courage to do it. This is the way it is. When you get guidance to let go of something, it's sort of like a time warning that says, 'You have ten days left. After that, your angel's going to do it.' So, the desire to hold on is not going to stop the process of change...You know that that's true.

-------- Caroline Myss

There is something to be said for being ripe. And I was ripe for this journey! That is an expression that I have used for years as I talk to clients about their readiness for change. Clients have inevitably come to me in various states, with multiple explanations for their problems. They yearn to feel better. Yet, I could tell within an hour whether or not they were really there to change *themselves*, if they expected *me* to "fix" them, or more commonly, if they still believed that *someone else* around them needed to change in order for them to be happy. When I sensed the individual (or couple) had arrived to ask me to help guide them to their *own* rediscovery, I knew they were ripe. It was as easy as tapping a cantaloupe or squeezing a mango.

When I embarked on my adventure in September, I was definitely ripe. Perhaps I was even a bit overripe, as I tend to endure pain and cling to the vine even after it's time to cut myself loose. This tendency to hold too tightly sometimes evolves because we are reacting from childhood training. Some of us learned to remain loyal in unhealthy situations or relationships long past the time when loyalty is called for. If we grew up in homes where we witnessed emotional or verbal abuse, for instance, a common tendency is to endure that same type of abuse in our adult relationships. We easily slip back into these patterns without realizing the harm we're inflicting on ourselves. This may manifest as staying in a job where we've been under-stimulated, under-appreciated or under-paid for way too long. At times it shows up as we remain in an unhealthy marriage, continuing to perform some form of resuscitation on our lifeless relationship, even though our "couple heart monitor" has gone flat and we no longer hear beeping.

Abroad is the place where we stay up
late, follow impulse and find ourselves
as wide open as when we are in love.

----- *Pico Iyer*

17

When you contemplate whether you are ready for change, a good metaphor to consider comes from great winemakers. As sleek, fast trains carried me through beautiful vineyards in France and Germany during my journey, I reflected on some of the lessons I had learned from listening to the wine experts. Those who pick grapes for the best wines tell us that impeccable timing is essential, that the grapes must be perfectly ripe - not picking them too early or too late - and of course a lot of hard work precedes the manifestation of the finished product. At times, impatient human nature tends to pick fruit off the vine too prematurely, while it is also our nature to procrastinate in taking risks in our own lives that lead to necessary and beneficial changes.

The day I began my journey, I left my home in Colorado to travel to Orlando to visit my son and leave my precious cat, 17 year-old Zippy. I was simply amazed at the incredible fear I felt. Since high school I had been looking forward to spending an extended period of time in Europe. Leaving the security of my home and precious belongings (family heirlooms, no less....what would my mother say if she knew?) was surprisingly difficult for me. At least at that point in time, what was familiar gave me the *illusion* of feeling secure. Much to my surprise and delight, however, I actually got in my car and drove off. Funny thing was that Colorado remained the same old place, just fine without me. The mountains didn't even budge. But, as I traveled across the U.S. visiting family and friends here and there and spending some time with my two children, my fear subsided and I felt a twinge of excitement again.

18

The irony is that the person not taking risks feels the same amount of fear as the person who regularly takes risks. The non-risk-taker simply feels the same amount of fear over trivial things.

----- *Peter McWilliams*

Then the time came to be alone. My daughter and son said good-bye to me and wished me a bon voyage. Their lives continued on as normal, although a piece of me sensed that they felt just a bit apprehensive about their mom flying off into the wild blue yonder. A mere acquaintance dropped me off at the Orlando airport. She seemed to notice my lack of friendly communication and some irritability, as it appeared to me the car was in slow motion. I was certain this must be a bad dream. There was *no one* to encourage, or nudge, me on to that plane leaving my country from Miami...only the momentum and efforts of my own self. I can't even describe the reluctance and fear I felt. My normal sunny and happy demeanor had transformed to a look of gloom and numbness, as I aimlessly sipped a cup of cold, weak coffee. Long after they announced the plane was boarding, I sat motionless, feeling as if a gigantic magnet was holding me to the seat, a mere 20 feet from the door through which I had to pass physically -- and mentally -- to board that plane. If I had known why I was going ---or where--- if there were only a concrete goal.....

Just because I was ripe and ready for change didn't mean I didn't feel great anxiety.

The strangest thought was penetrating my entire being, over and over: I had flunked the first 50 years of life's lessons and I was being sent somewhere, I imagined it must be somewhere like hell, to **finally** learn what I hadn't been able to grasp in the first half century! Going off alone into the unknown felt like the worse punishment I'd ever had to endure. I wasn't even raised Catholic, yet it felt like I was being sent away somewhere to "do penance" because I just hadn't gotten it. It?? Life, I suppose.

Courage is as often the outcome of despair as hope; in the one case we have nothing to lose, in the other, all to gain.

----- Diane DePoitiers

Tools for Navigating Through Your Fears

- Using my analogy about the "ripeness" of people to change and heal, how ripe do you think you are at this point in time regarding your desire to navigate through your fears?

  totally

- What lengths are you willing to go to in order to work on your fears to promote substantial and long-lasting change?

  Name it!
  Name them!

- When I was talking about my feelings while flying from Miami to London, I mentioned that I felt like I had flunked the first 50 years of my life and was being sent somewhere to re-learn some of the lessons I missed. If you decided to give yourself a "review" for your life up to this point, what comments would you make about what you have:
  - Learned

  I am giving / nurturing myself & others

  - take time before trusting men
  - I can survive & thrive!
  - I have a strong work ethic
  very bright, & good analytically

- ability to jump off windowsills on way down

- **Gained**
  - compassion for myself & others
  - financial independence

Mom & Dad not protecting me from Mr. Hulick

-people pleaser

- **Disliked**
  - failed marriages & relationships w/ men
  - Mr. Hulick

- **Liked**
  - ability to laugh often & heartily!

- **Truly valued**
  - ability to keep getting up & moving forward

- And what would you say about your own self image? For example, where would you rank yourself on a scale from self-loathing to unconditional self love?

I love myself.
I am worthy.
I am perfect in God's eyes.

CHAPTER FOUR

FLYING BY THE SEAT OF YOUR PANTS

*And the day came when the risk to
remain tight in a bud was more painful than the risk it took to blossom.*

----- *Author unknown*

Once on that plane, I pulled out some of my trusted words of wisdom both in book and on tapes, like a child holding tight to her well-worn stuffed animal. One of those books was Levoy's *Callings,* in which he warns his readers about the "Mach I phenomenon" that astronauts experience as they embark on their flights and begin to ascend. The shaking and trembling is almost unbearable. The fear pulsing throughout my body and heart shook me just like I was an astronaut. My logical side kept rationalizing, insisting that my journey was much, much safer than space travel. But risk-taking is very relative, what is fearful to one person is not to another. My fear felt vivid and intensely real. I felt like I was headed for Mars! Levoy also writes that "the entrée into enlightenment comes with a side order of holy terror, and one must have the appetite for it." At that moment, my appetite for adventure had turned to nausea!

23

Just when I was debating how I might turn around at Heathrow Airport in London and get on the next available flight back to Miami, I very cautiously and slowly opened the shade on the airplane window. I sat and peered out at the darkest sky and the most brilliant stars I had ever seen. It was breathtaking!

Stars have always been a source of comfort to me. Times when I've felt lost and alone, I have had the stars to light my way. Whether it is spending serene hours by myself in Colorado's Rocky Mountain National Park, or camping in the wilderness with my children, gazing at those sparkling lights in the heavens brings me incredible peace. Now they were the Universe's first obvious gift to me. They always represent a constant for me, a reassurance that *all is well*. And smack in the middle of the sky, full of dazzling lights twinkling down on me, were ten stars in the perfect shape of an arrow. It was pointing up. I read that as a sign to keep my inner vision directed upward, higher…to let go of the mundane, everyday *stuff* and trust in something much more significant.

> *Daring ideas are like chessmen*
> *moved forward; they may be beaten,*
> *but they may start a winning game.*
> ----- *Johann Wolfgang von Goethe*

After a few more hours of restless attempts to sleep, I again poked my eyes through the darkness of what seemed to be a dream, and I was able to *just* glimpse sunlight touching the earth's edge. This sight gave me a thrill that was worth the price of the airfare. The huge world below me was turning, and the light I had been praying for appeared...first outside along the horizon, then in my heart. Seeing the sun there, as it *always* is, and thinking of all the people, critters and plants living on this now visible globe, granted me a *knowing,* reassured me, that we are all connected and nothing is separate. Everything just continues, flows, constantly moves, forever grows and changes. Life is all together ONE. I truly began to understand the teachings in the book study I had struggled with at times over the past few years. *A Course in Miracles* published by the Foundation for Inner Peace says that there are no separate minds or bodies. The illusions with which I live, even the preposterous belief that it is night when it is dark, day when it is light, suddenly vanished. It is always light somewhere!

And merely because I don't **see** something, doesn't mean it isn't there.

When you resist a difficulty, you
antagonize it, and it hits back.

----- *Emmet Fox*

These are ideas I'd been working on believing for most of my adult life. I had strongly believed for some time that when I am in a "dark" time of my life, my belief in a Higher Intelligence enables me to trust that my challenge is part of the Divine Design of my life and that light will appear. But now I saw even further beyond belief to a **knowing,** as Divine Order unfolded right before my eyes. It was *grand*! And I finally felt peace and an understanding that I wasn't supposed to turn around and return to what *seemed* to be security and safety at "home." I *was* home, within myself, and all was very well indeed.

As we prepare to make changes in our lives, in addition to working through our own fears, we frequently encounter the obstacle of bumping up against other people's fears. These often show up as worry and concern, even an opportunity to pass judgment about what we are planning to do. Best selling author and inspirational speaker, Wayne Dyer, has been an influential mentor of mine for 25 years. He encourages us to live fully and joyfully by drawing from the Spiritual strength within us. One belief he teaches is that it is important to be independent of the good opinion of others. I was well trained by family and society to be an excellent people pleaser. Asking me to detach from others' viewpoints of how I should live my life was at first a difficult task to tackle, but one I wanted to change. I am happy to report that because I've truly worked on altering this behavior, I've made great strides in reducing my people pleasing tendencies. Practice and determination *can* promote change!

Let me listen to me and not to them.

----- *Gertrude Stein*

Prior to my departure, when I began sharing with friends and family about my planned journey, I heard many of their voices and opinions, but mostly their own fears, as their well-intended counsel was that I reconsider my decision:

"You're either really stupid or very brave."
"I heard of someone in Europe who was kidnapped and they never found her again."
"They gas people on the trains in Europe, you know, and rob them."
"They're having a gas shortage over there right now and people are rioting."
"You know your cat's going to die while you're over there."
"You can't go on this trip, Susie, because it is very dangerous, expensive and how can you compete with the beautiful, young, large breasted women in France, and besides you won't meet any rich men traveling in the style you will be going." (this was my favorite, since I was hoping simply to meet *myself* on this journey, not men!)

I was quite aware of my *own* fears and trepidations. I wasn't afraid I was going to die, in fact, the plane going down over the Atlantic that first night would have been a welcome relief from my anxiety! I was afraid of being alone, totally alone with myself, with nothing secure, familiar or comforting around me. I was choosing to displace myself by heading into unknown and unfamiliar territory, facing the unpredictable.

Facing myself.

All of my trepidations did help me understand why it is so difficult for all of us to make changes in our lives. Yet, I knew deep within me that change is the only constant I've had in my life and one of the only guarantees in this entire world.

> *Most people don't know that there*
> *are angels whose only job is to make*
> *sure you don't get too comfortable*
> *and fall asleep and miss your life.*
>
> ----- *Brian Andreas*

Tools for Navigating Through Your Fears

- Did you relate to my Mach I experience when I felt so much fear leaving the country? If so, when, where, and what was your experience and can you describe your feelings of fear?

- What resources do you use that bring you inner peace and calm when you are experiencing anxiety? It helps to list your strengths, past experiences and methods for finding serenity.

  — hot baths
  — viewing life as an adventure
  — life is like a tree — each choice/decision takes us out some branch — & there are loads of branches.

- Who in your life tends to share their fears, trepidations, negativity with your when you are contemplating change or discussing your dreams and desires? How do you react to them and how can you turn the situation into a positive for *you*? Are you able to let their fears be *theirs* and not become yours, too?

  Used to be Mom.
  Accept that she chooses to live in a box
  I choose life's adventures outside the box

- When inexperienced riders get ready to mount their horses, helpful people sometimes cup their hands together, offering to give the rider a boost or a "leg-up" to assist them in getting up in the saddle and ready to go! We can also think of supportive, encouraging people in our lives as "leg-up

29

people." Name three such people in your life, and don't forget to ask them for a leg-up when you need one. If you can't name any such support in your life now, begin thinking of who might be in your life that could become such a person when you need a leg-up.

Barry

Beth

Claudia

Andy

Bruce

Stephanie

Bonnie

John Sobol

Matthew

No longer - locket
Dick
Dad
Mom

Mark

CHAPTER FIVE

COURAGE EXPANDS WITH USE

Don't be afraid your life will end.
Be afraid that it will never begin.

----- *Grace Hansen*

The overall lessons of my *life* journey have seemed to focus on my ability to let go and trust in my Source. My belief about my Creator is that it is a God-force, a loving power that is only good. It is that part of me that is much wiser than my human self, or the superficial me that worries, judges, resents, and feels inadequate and guilty. I encourage each of you to begin asking yourself this question: "What has designed my life?" I invite you to explore what is holding you back, why you allow yourself to settle or stagnate when deep inside you feel intense longing to be more because you know you *are* more. As you begin to ask yourself and experiment with these questions, parts of you that have remained dormant for too long will begin to stir.

This exploration can result in you experiencing some of the same benefits I did during my trip when I used my courage to expand my comfort zone. I do not wish upon you my life, but I do wish for you what my journey brought to me. *The rewards of my trip were of incredible value to me.* I felt a hungry passion for life and respect for myself again. As I continued on, facing rather than avoiding my fears, their power over me diminished and I began experiencing bliss in ordinary, everyday events. I appreciated simplicity while not accepting mediocrity. I gained enormous confidence and feelings of worthiness. I began liking myself more and valuing who and what I am. My joy increased as my fear and anger decreased. I felt less judgmental and practiced more patience toward others. I rediscovered a strength that I believe has always been within me, but I now felt a calm reassurance that the source of it is an always-present Power that is beyond my human self. And, finally, I began to embrace that peace that passes understanding that I'd only heard about before.

People do not crave meaning,
they crave aliveness!

----- *Joseph Campbell*

Many psychotherapists have various theories to help their clients increase self-esteem. The one I believe to be the most effective, which I practice myself, is risk-taking behavior. Fear diminishes as we take actions outside our comfort zones, which in turn improves our feelings of self-regard. I can see that the times throughout my entire life when I've mustered up the courage to take risks were the most exhilarating, rewarding, confidence-building and fun. I also felt the most alive and bursting with happiness at those moments as well.

Human beings are born to explore, expand, grow and enjoy life to the utmost. Playing it safe, settling or stagnating seems to go against our very nature, and the resulting feeling is usually inadequacy. This pattern is obvious as I watch my clients risk-take, or stay stuck. If, for example, someone tells me they are in an unsatisfactory marriage and they choose to do nothing about it, it begins to erode their feelings of worthiness. We don't like ourselves much when we know we are unhappy, yet continue with more of what is at the root of the unhappiness.

One indication that you are longing to set free a trapped part of you is observing your reaction to a book or movie character, perhaps identifying someone as your heroine or hero. For over 30 years, Maude has been my heroine. She's a 79 year-old plunky, spirited woman who *loves* life to the utmost, as she grabs all the gusto she can, as well as your heart, in *Herold and Maude*. In this 1970's produced classic film written by Colin Higgins, Maude appreciates and values the little, ordinary thrills and adventures in everyday life. Within a few short days she teaches her young, but terribly depressed and emotionally-devoid friend Herold, some lessons about life that I value and appreciate, as well. As we watch Maude, we learn how to risk more, worry less about what others think and do "something new each day." As Maude says, "After all we're given life to find it out, it doesn't last forever."

Life shrinks or expands in
proportion to one's courage.

----- *Anais Nin*

Maude also describes people who appear half dead, while still very much physically alive, to morose Herold. "Yes, I understand. A lot of people enjoy being dead. But they're not dead, really. They're just backing away from life. They're players, but they think life is a practice game and they'll save themselves for later. So they sit on the bench, and the only championship they'll ever see goes on before them. The clock ticks away the quarters. At any moment they can join in -- go on, guys! Reach out! Take a chance! Get hurt, maybe. But play as well as you can. Otherwise, you'll have nothing to talk about in the locker room."

Wouldn't *you* like to have many blissful tales to talk about in the locker room?

As I mentioned earlier, fear is the major roadblock on the path to serenity. It comes in such a variety of shapes and sizes and is disguised so well that we usually don't recognize it (how many of us express anger when we are really scared -- or think that worry thoughts can actually control an event, or make/ prevent something from happening?). Being anxious continually robs us of happiness and joy, a deep, basic joy that I describe as BLISS. Bliss is more than temporary pleasure stemming from a momentary event, but rather a profound feeling within us that resounds throughout our entire being. When you're blissful, you know it.

Whatever there be of progress in life, comes not through adaptation, but through daring. The whole logic of the Universe is contained in daring, in creating from the flimsiest, slenderest support.

----- Henry Miller

Sadly, not many of us truly feel blissful very often. How many times have you really experienced bliss in your life? Count them. Where were you? Were you alone or with someone? What were you doing? What did it feel like? What did it do for you? Did you enjoy it or did it feel a bit strange for you? I've given this assignment to clients, and not many can name many blissful moments in their life.

I believe that a Loving Energy (you name it whatever you want) created us to be happy. Sacrifice, suffering and misery don't fit into that model. Neither do fretting, anxiety, worry or obsessing about possible disasters. Does that mean we don't experience problems? Of course we do! But, what I am suggesting is that you begin to exchange your old "worry paradigm," the one that you learned from society or family, for a new plan that reassures you continually that

you do deserve to feel blissful. Simply beginning to believe that is a start. It stands to reason: if you know you are an extension of the Love that created you, and if you believe that Creator is good, then *your* essence is Goodness as well. As you expand your awareness, experiment with your thoughts and see yourself as a piece of the Goodness, you will begin choosing trust over fear more and more often. You will begin to notice a glow and delightful calm within yourself. Humans do not waste time or energy on worry when they are in a blissful state.

The choice is always ours to make, in each and every moment.
Which are you choosing in this very moment...fear or happiness?

The subjects of perspective and letting go are important to this discussion as well, and as you read on further you will learn more about those.

> *Lose this day loitering – 'twill be*
> *the same story tomorrow and the*
> *next more dilatory. Each decision*
> *brings its own delays. And days*
> *are lost lamenting o'er lost days.*
> *Are you in earnest? Seize this*
> *very minute—Boldness has genius,*
> *power and magic in it!*
> ----- *Johann Wolfgang von Goethe*

36

Tools for Navigating Through Your Fears

- Are you only <u>partially</u> glimpsing that which you really want in your life? If so, what price are you personally paying for remaining discontent?

  - days lost in depression
  - playing victim instead of fearless wonder

- When you contemplate those last questions, what is your spontaneous reaction to the phrase, "that which you really want?" What is that for you? Be as specific as possible and use extra paper if necessary.

  live simply
  love much
  laugh often
  leave a mark

  stay financially independent
  find pleasure & beauty in every day

- What do you suspect are the reasons you have settled for less than you deserve in the past (or presently)? Why do you think you stagnate when you know you are capable of so much more? Try not to get into blaming others or circumstances, but rather take complete responsibility for this yourself. (i.e. give <u>your</u> reaction to what your father might say if you decide to quit college to travel the world) The key here

because I let a fear dominate
unimportant values
don't trust my gut

is to accept responsibility, *without blaming yourself* or falling into self-degradation, and allow that sense of responsibility to lead you instead to self-empowerment.

- What character in a book or movie have you related to, wanted to be more like or perhaps felt envious of? What was it specifically that that person had that you were longing for?

related to — Scarlet O'Hard
respect — Katharine Hepburn
Meryl Streep,
strong, independent

- Name one story that you would like to be able to talk about in the "locker room," (it can be an event that already occurred or a dream you have).

travels w/ Mom

dream
hike all the trails
in RMNP

CHAPTER SIX

WHEN YOUR BOAT NEEDS ROCKING

It's a sad day when you find out
that it's not accident or time or
fortune but just yourself that kept
things from you.

----- *Lillian Hellman*

As my self-expansion journey in Europe continued, gifts from the Universe poured into my life on a daily basis. But, as I look back on it now, I think it was simply my ability to tune into each present moment and my expanded awareness that had changed. They were undoubtedly there all along. Becoming still, tuning out the world and taking time each day to connect to my Divine Source in silence opened me up to seeing, hearing and experiencing **more**. More of everything life has to offer.

As I began to consciously "practice the Presence," or feel connected to my Higher Power on a more regular basis, one of the changes I noticed was synchronicities occurring more regularly. People, events and circumstances began showing up just as if they'd been given the cues and were well-rehearsed and ready to perform. I became increasingly sensitive, more receptive, and as I began to relax and trust myself and the internal Radar system that seemed to be working for me, my life began to flow more easily.

I have come to believe that life just goes more smoothly -- that events, people, circumstances fall into place -- as we open ourselves up to the natural order of life, to the energy that drives everything and is everywhere in this Universe. It is that force which connects us all. As I recalled the stars, earth and sun rising that first morning on my journey, I began to feel at one with that energy and began cooperating with it by *allowing* it to work for me. Letting go suddenly felt much more peaceful than resisting.

Don't get your knickers in a knot.
Nothing is solved, and it just makes
you walk funny.

----- *Kathryn Carpenter*

As I noticed little things begin to fall in place, *it became a delightful challenge to notice, allow and practice accepting.* For example, about one week after my arrival in Europe, I was staying in a teensy, quaint room in Edinburgh, Scotland, and I just happened to catch the end of a TV special on Silicon Valley, California. The host was interviewing a mother who was joyfully recalling when her daughter was asked who she looked up to most, and she replied "My

mother." The woman said this comment had made he
struggles as a parent worthwhile. When she heard her d
knew she wasn't doing this all of this for herself.

Bells and whistles immediately went off in my head. I realized
that I was facing this challenge of feeling isolated -- far away from the
familiar and secure, traveling alone in .foreign countries -- in order to
not only find myself, but somehow to help my family, friends and
clients as well. There were two who were watching me most closely.
The two who would certainly see evidence of the outcome of this
journey. The two for whom I hoped to learn so I could teach. My two
children. I knew after hearing the woman interviewed that when I had
thoughts of backing out at the last moment, when I wanted to chicken
out and give up, I hadn't backed out because I needed to go through
this for them too. I wanted to do this for their sake, as well as mine. I
wanted to be a good role model. Not just talk the talk, but walk the
walk, as well. As I was striving to live more fully, taking risks that
would increase my self-confidence, choosing an abundant life rather
than a fear-restricted one, I knew they were watching and learning.

When the waters get too calm, the
boat needs a little rocking.

----- *Jocelyn Holst*
My Wise Daughter

One of the great things about parent/child relationships is that we, as parents, also learn from our children! One of my biggest fans and one of the people who had encouraged me unconditionally to make this journey was my 23 year-old daughter. Although she seems to have taken me down from the pedestal that most kids as they're growing up have their parents on, she now sees me as I am and still believes in me. That feels great! When she was just out of high school and completely, far away from home for the first time, I received a letter from her that I keep to re-read and treat myself to now and then. She was encouraging me to liberate myself from a lifestyle that had been stagnant, boring and unfulfilling for quite awhile. Her words were reminding me that, although going with the flow can be great, getting stuck in the mud is not, and flowing means going – not standing still. I can still recall her wisdom:

"God's heart is within your own, so trust what it tells you. When the waters get <u>too</u> calm, the boat needs a little rocking. Perhaps you won't change the world, but you'll certainly change everyone's life you encounter, which is kind of like changing the world! So GO FOR IT, whatever 'it' may be."

My son's words of wisdom were incredible as well. I was sharing with him prior to my departure some of the cautious comments people had made to me regarding my upcoming journey. "Yeah, Mom," he replied, "and you could also stay home and never take any major risks, walk out your front door some day and be hit by a bus!" I recalled both of their wise thoughts throughout my trip when I doubted what I was doing and whether or not I could continue.

Everything in life can be frightening *if we hold to the belief that it is*. The kind of support I received from my children, before and during my trip, helped me continue on. Plus, I knew from years of counseling that there were many clients and others, perhaps *you*, who were needing to learn similar lessons, gain insight as I was, so I was eager to figure out at least a bit of life for many. It is important to surround yourself with cheerleaders, optimists and other courageous people who will support and encourage you, especially when you are in the midst of change and fear seems to be lurking at every turn.

> *Don't refuse to go on an occasional wild goose chase; that is what wild geese are made for.*
>
> ----- *Henry S. Haskins*

Tools for Navigating Through Your Fears

- How many times have you really experienced *bliss* in your life? Where were you, were you alone or with another person, what were you doing, and what did it feel like? Writing about this will help you recall how great it is to feel blissful!

watching snow fall inside
listening to wind through trees

- hiking w/a friend in the mountains
- walking on a beach
- listening to the water go by while sailing

43

- When you're thinking about your personal boat being stuck in the mud, how would you describe that for *you*? What is keeping you stuck? What choices are you making that contribute to your stagnation? And what is in the boat that you desire to row forward?

- wanting something that does not yet exist.
eg. Victor's values & integrity
- care of & compassion for myself & others
- strength to trust my gut/intuition

- What limiting, anxiety-producing beliefs are you holding onto that keep you from realizing your potential? The first step to changing a behavior or limiting belief is to admit it's there. Take five minutes, NOW and in the quiet stillness, to ask yourself "What would I like to do with these beliefs?" (Be honest with yourself...if you're not ready to let them go, say so.)

Have the strength & courage to value myself. divorce Victor with love

CHAPTER SEVEN

WHEN PUSH NEEDS A LITTLE SHOVE

When your ship, long moored in
harbour, gives you the illusion of
being a house...put out to sea! Save
your boat's journeying soul, and your
own pilgrim soul, cost what it may.
----- Brazilian Archbishop Helder Camara

After one week into my journey, I was still asking this question on a regular basis. "What is it I am here for?" I began to trust that answers would come, but I didn't know when they would or how they would appear. I was flying by the seat of my pants and moving through this experience on pure faith, trusting my Divine Radar as I moved into each new moment. Quieting my mind, maintaining a sense of awareness and being vigilant to the Spirit within me helped me read that inner Radar.

As I made my way from northern England to the Isle of Wight off the south coast, I dug into my reservoirs of physical and emotional strength that up until this point, I didn't even know I had. I first discovered these reserves while navigating my way through the

Underground, the London subway system. I picked an unusually busy day to travel when there was a national football championship being played and huge crowds swarmed everywhere. To add to the confusion, many major stops were closed and escalators halted due to repairs.

Before I knew it I was changing trains again, hauling two heavy backpacks up one very long flight of stairs, four stories high, in record time with hundreds of people trampling right on my heels! About half way up the steps, I glanced over my shoulder and saw a blur of not-so-happy faces. This motivated me to dig even deeper. Somehow I felt like I was the victim in a Roadrunner cartoon, as I recalled poor Wiley Coyote encountering some surprising object head-on as he was innocently going about his business. The amusing image of me being flattened by polite Brits as they apologized and ran over me kept me going. After purchasing a few gifts for my family, my backpacks felt like two-ton rocks, and all I could consider in the moment were silly, self-condemning thoughts of why I had weighted myself down. I was not only frightened that I was incapable of physically handling the challenge, but I also feared not being able to negotiate my way through the Underground detours.

The human race has one really effect-
tive weapon, and that is laughter.

----- *Mark Twain*

As my petite, five-foot-one-inch frame successfully arrived at the top of the staircase, my second challenge came up. I had to figure out how to walk to the next stop since the one I needed was closed. Thankfully, a kind woman gave me detailed directions, and I made my way through the drizzle to the Waterloo Train Station. After standing in a long line to buy the cheapest train ticket available, I finally managed to find the right train track, car and seat, on time, while lugging all those thoughtful gifts with me every step of the way. With perspiration covering my body, I gratefully slipped into my seat. I then slyly attempted to rearrange my hidden waist-pack under my shirt, while realizing that I must certainly be a sight to behold. As I pulled my hands out from under my shirt, I looked up and into the eyes of a gorgeous man (I soon discovered he was Scottish, wouldn't you know it, they take my breath away!). I gently wiped the sweat from my forehead, smiled slightly, contained my embarrassment as much as possible and uttered a friendly American hello.

The moral of this story? Walking through fears, facing physical and emotional challenges, is not necessarily *easy*. We don't always have clear direction or know exactly what to do next. *Enjoying the unknown is called embracing the mystery of life.* You decide. You can choose to be afraid and let that limit you, or you can forge ahead, do what you fear and delight in uncovering the mystery!

As Mark Twain reminds us, don't forget to utilize one of the most fabulous gifts you've been given in life – *your humor.* It saw me through many embarrassing circumstances!

For most men life is a search for the proper
manila envelope in which to get themselves filed.

----- *Clifton Fadiman*

Besides humor, as I traveled about and managed my way through challenges, I also recalled stories and wisdom shared by wonderful mentors I've had. Many years ago when I was whining one day, a former supervisor remarked, "Who told you, Susie, that life was a bowl of cherries?" In other words, buck up and handle it, not from a position of fear, but rather from that of strength. If ever I began feeling self-pity or loneliness, I would remind myself to simply face up to my feelings and do something about them. (By the way, writing a list of things you are grateful for really helps dissolve self-pity.)

This physical journey was representative of my inner journey. I slowly began confronting my wandering thoughts and fears. I knew that I wanted to be able to transfer what I was learning about myself by going away, to other areas of my life. My inner urging to take this trip included desires to gain much more than time away, as I wanted to increase the richness of my life at home. I had not been living up to my potential, was feeling underutilized and I was hoping that lessons learned on this journey would inspire me to be more. More of what I am here on this planet to be.

I realized as time went by that traveling by myself, in a foreign country, is entirely different than doing it with others. I had no one to rely on but myself. It was frightening for me, just as it can be for most people, but it was also one of the main points of fear I was forging through. Many of the people I have counseled have told me that they would be more comfortable if they could somehow obtain a "written guarantee" for their life, especially about major decisions they were in the process of making. I, too, sometimes wish there were assurances, such as a certain person always being there for me, or that I won't starve, or that my loved ones and I will always be safe and secure. I've checked many government sources, countless libraries and many expensive stores for such guarantees.... haven't found one yet! But there is great news. *All the assurance you need is within you.*

You gotta have heart, all you really need is heart.
When the odds are saying you'll never win, that's
when the grin should start. You gotta have hope,
mustn't sit around and mope. Nothing's half as bad
as it would appear, wait 'til next year and hope....
It's fine to be a genius of course, but keep that old
horse before the cart. First, you gotta have heart!

----- Richard Adler and Jerry Ross
"You Gotta Have Heart"
from "Damn Yankees"

Tools for Navigating Through Your Fears

- Including humor, what other "weapons" do you possess, or what coping strategies do you use, to help get you through tough times, stressful or frightening events? (i.e. gardening, painting, nature walks, dancing, talking to friends, etc.)

  — talking to friends
  — traveling somewhere fun
  — quiet time outdoors
  — receiving love & affection from my pups

- Think of a time when you faced either a physical, intellectual or emotional challenge that you emerged from feeling great about yourself. What, specifically, do you think contributed to your improved self-image?

  — ending my relationship with Mr. Hulick
  — believing I am worthy

CHAPTER EIGHT

SHOULDA, COULDA, WOULDA

I'm not afraid of storms, for I am
learning how to sail my ship.

----- *Louisa May Alcott*

One of my lifelong fears is water. I rationalize that fear by reminding myself that it only includes water above my head! Traveling across the wind-blown sea from Portsmouth to the Isle of Wight in a small catamaran was yet another step in forging through my anxieties. As I entered the craft, I carefully checked out locations of life preservers, plotting my escape plan. *Just in case.* I drew in a deep breath, remembered to trust my Higher Power (and the captain) and reminded myself that the only way to navigate through fears is to face them.

To my delight, the trip was actually pleasant and I loved the exhilaration I felt as we sped across the bouncy water. My reason for braving the rough waters to go to the Isle was because my great-great-great grandfather Jonas Daish was born and lived on the island for years, and there is an old hotel still in use named The Daish Hotel, where I was able to stay. I wanted to travel there to research our family roots and to share this information with my mother and aunt who both love studying our heritage, but could not themselves travel.

Upon arriving on the beautiful Isle of Wight, I felt a bit like Alice in Wonderland. I saw myself transformed into a yet unknown fairy tale. Tiny thatched-roofed houses line the narrow roads that coil around Old Shanklin Village, while paths leading from the main road escort you to the English Channel, or as the locals call it, the sea. The sea bounces up against huge, white cliffs resembling the White Cliffs of Dover I'd seen in movies. It is a picturesque setting. Quaint reminder of days of yore. Many authors and artists have spent time drawing inspiration from this isle -- Longfellow, Darwin, Keats, to name a few.

While rain poured down on the Isle, I pored through the local library for clues about my family. My research also included talking to the experts at the county seat and asking locals for information. One kind resident suggested I take a walk to the town cemetery to dig further for my heritage. The walk itself was a sensory treat, despite the cold and rain. I examined *each* headstone, braving the eerie, secluded setting with the hope of coming across a link to my past. Viewing the tombstones, I discovered stories of many people, some who could have been related. What struck me were the young ages at which these villagers had died. Especially the women, since they were about my age. It surprised me somehow when I realized how many generations had lived and died in less than 200 years. I felt sad thinking that their stories, loves, passions, favorite activities and beliefs were lost in time and no longer cared about in the present. I think their time here probably whizzed by just as it does for us!

You don't get to choose how you're going to die. Or when. You can only decide how you're going to live. Now.

----- *Joan Baez*

As I strolled down paths that were *exactly* those my ancestors had once walked, I had an incredibly overwhelming dose of mortality therapy. The perspective that I gained from examining my roots, walking those paths, made me question what I was doing with my own life. *It invited me to be more.* After 50 years of incomplete living, it was time to quit frittering my life away. Time to move beyond petty details and distractions and get on with living a richer, more meaningful life. I felt motivated to dig deeper into the passion I had suppressed, to find aliveness again. I didn't feel like playing small any longer.

Stephen Covey in his book *The Seven Habits of Highly Effective People* suggests that each of us should imagine his/her own funeral and imagine what people would say about us. These could include family members, co-workers, members of our community and church. In other words, when you do get to the end, will you be able to gleefully announce, "I'm all used up and delighted with the way it happened!" Or will you notice the regrets and say, "Gee I wish I had loved more, played more, worried less, traveled more, lightened up, complained less or ………you name it." Yes, try to name it now.

In the beginning of the film "City of Angels," an angel has come to help transition the young girl who is dying. As they are walking down the hospital corridor to the light at the end, he asks her,

"What did you like best about it?"

That is an important question to ask yourself. Your answer can be very telling. Listen closely. I had a female friend in the late 1960's (when many women were still fairly traditional housewives) who told me that when she died she did *not* want on her tombstone, "This woman really kept a clean house." I still carry the memory of it because it made such an impact. It made me think about what I would like written on my tombstone. I agree that it wouldn't be that I spent my life cleaning! I would want it to have something to do with the joy I have found in living and loving fully, without constraint. Perhaps mine would read: "Susie was a courageous, adventurous woman who loved with joyful freedom, savored each moment completely, abandoned fears to gleefully embrace all of life, treasured the richness of each adventure and found delight in the mystery of all."

What about yours?

I want to live, I want to grow, I
want to see, I want to know, I
want to share what I can give,
I want to be, I want to live.

----- *John Denver*
From "I Want to Live"

Sadly, we humans act as if we have a thousand years to live. Some of us procrastinate, thinking we will get around to it "some day." Some of us put off telling those we love how much we truly adore them. Others stay in that job that is under-stimulating and unfulfilling. Then others deny themselves their dream trip to some exotic place they've always wanted to visit. Even worse is when our lack of boldness prevents us from even venturing into the possibility of a relationship.

According to the friends and clients I've listened to, emotional risks seem to be the most frightening, because matters of the heart are so delicate. Love can easily bruise. Heartaches penetrate deeply. I heard many years ago that "hurt people hurt people." Many of us feel vulnerable, afraid after we've suffered a heartbreak. We often feel let down or betrayed when we believe that someone we loved and trusted misused that trust. Once hurt, we guard our emotional wound carefully. That lends itself to hurting others, which in turn causes more of the same, and on and on it goes. Hurt people hurt people.

Therefore, many of us become terrified of love. As my sister once said, "Love is not what makes the world go 'round, but it does make the ride worthwhile!" If we could only see that the fear of taking a risk with love is *our* loss. We end up betraying ourselves by cutting ourselves off from that within us that longs to love and be loved. Not being loving is contrary to our true nature. Ask yourself and take time to ponder some time within the next 72 hours: Have I allowed a heartache to trap me in fear to the point that I am closed off from grasping what makes my ride worthwhile? Have I let fear control me so that I am denying myself one of the greatest joys in life?

Then we hit the half-way point of life. The challenge of mid-life. The lessons of having lived through 40 plus years of life are tough for most of us to swallow, as our culture continues to value youth over aging. But there are gifts in those lessons. How else is it going to sink in that we don't have a thousand years here to just mess around? I used to think "mid-life crisis" was a ridiculous expression that merely described an ex-husband of a scorned woman who drives a cute, sporty car and chases younger women. Then I got my little red sports car and began dating a younger man. Using my skills as a therapist, I tried to figure out what my behavior was telling me.

What I realized is that after years of distracting myself with wonderful society-sanctioned diversions, (like focusing on my children, men, my work, beauty products that promise the fountain of youth, and on and on) I think I'm beginning to see the light peeking in through the door of my carefully self-furrowed cave! A few such gifts

I've received from "life experience" are: don't sweat the small stuff, remember that "this too shall pass," and live more in the present moment rather than the past or future.

Dan Fogelburg reminds us in his song, "Run For the Roses," that it's time to get on with living. "It's run for the roses as fast as you can. Your fate is delivered, your moment's at hand. It's the chance of a lifetime in a lifetime of chance. And it's high time you joined in the dance. Yes, it's high time you joined in the dance."

Live every day as if it were your last,
because one of these days it will be.
----- *Jeremy Schwartz*

It's high time we all start dancing. What is *your* favorite "dance," and why do you stand on the sidelines watching others kick up their heels and only dream of doing that yourself? What keeps you from getting out there on the dance floor? By the time we've had 40 or more years of preparation for living fully, hopefully one of life's gifts to us is not worrying so much about looking foolish. Who cares if you stumble through the dance steps?

Experts on grief and dying tell us that for many people facing a terminal situation their greatest regret is not what they did, but what they did *not* do during their life. There is nothing more disturbing or down-right sad than having regrets at any stage of life. The saddest thing is not that we die, but that we may have never fully lived. That we walked around half dead while we were alive. What causes this phenomenon, this kind of emotional death? I believe it is fear.

Perhaps many of our fears around death are actually created because down deep we're afraid we have not lived according to our dreams. In order to address these fears, it might be necessary to dig into our old treasure chest of dreams and, as difficult as it may be, bring out those old ideas, dust them off and ask ourselves if it is time to pursue a few. Perhaps looking at the old ones might trigger some enthusiasm for creating some new ones. The lock on our treasure chest is almost always fear.

Life is meant to be an adventure, enjoyable and full of love and laughter at every turn in the road. Sometimes that road is bumpy. But the more we travel the adventure road, the greater our ability to find the fun route over the rough spots. It would be so great if people could learn these lessons prior to midlife. I do not want to live vicariously through my children by watching them live out "my dreams." I do not want to *tell* my children to go out and live their lives with more pizzaz (because I did *not*). I want to show them, demonstrate for them, by being a courageous role model as they observe *me* blissfully off on yet another new adventure!

Sometimes you just have to take a
leap and build your wings on the
way down.

----- *Kobi Yamada*

Tools for Navigating Through Your Fears

- Contemplate what your own funeral would look/sound like. What would friends, family, co-workers or community/church members say about you? Pay attention to your initial gut reaction to your responses. Do any of these revelations inspire you to change any of your actions, thoughts, beliefs or feelings today? Or, does any part of this assignment stir up any regrets or resentments? If so, be specific and list them.

- If you were walking down a "hallway" toward the Light, how would you respond if your angel asked you, "What did you like best about it?" And how often do you allow yourself to revel in the joy of whatever you named as "best?"

- What would you like written on your tombstone? Write it down here.

CHAPTER NINE

MORTALITY THERAPY ENLIVENS

It's the heart afraid of breaking that
never learns to dance. It's the dream
afraid of waking that never takes a chance.
It's the one who won't be taken that cannot
seem to give, and the soul afraid of dying
that never learns to live.

----- *Amanda McBroom*
From "The Rose"

For years I have taught about looking at one's own mortality. Getting in touch with the concept that we don't live forever on this earthly plane. I realize this is not a popular subject, since many of us do not want to think about death, let alone talk out loud about it! For those of you that cringe from even the mention of the word, you might benefit from asking yourself how much joy in your life is being denied because of your fear of death. This could mean fear of your own death, the death of loved ones or perhaps even fear of the demise of your country.

One of the exercises that has helped me face my fear of death is strolling through cemeteries. Once I actually took the time to begin reading the tombstones and dates, and focused on the messages, it was then I learned valuable lessons. The number one lesson is: life is short. It goes so quickly. I think we need to remind ourselves of that on a regular basis. Instead, we tend to squander our time and our opportunities and take the extraordinary in the ordinary for granted far too often. It seems like such a loss to not be fully alive on all levels while our bodies are still ticking.

After humorist and author Erma Bombeck was diagnosed with terminal cancer, she wrote these touching words of wisdom as she looked back over a few of her regrets:

"I would have invited friends over to dinner, even if the carpet was stained and the sofa faded. I would have eaten the popcorn in the 'GOOD' living room and worried much less about the dirt when someone wanted to light a fire in the fireplace....I would never have insisted the car windows be rolled up on a summer day because my hair had just been teased and sprayed....I would have sat on the lawn with my children and not worried about grass stains....I would have gone to bed when I was sick instead of pretending the earth would go into a holding pattern if I weren't there for the day....When my kids kissed me impetuously I would never have said, 'Later. Now go get washed up for dinner.'"

I believe we can all learn from Erma's wisdom. How many times you have worried needlessly about stains on the carpet or if your hair looked perfect? When I reflect back on my life, these types of minor worries were absolutely worthless, in fact they contributed nothing to my serenity or joy.

The past is not only that which
happened but also that which
could have happened but did not.
----- Tess Gallagher

We don't live forever. Some of us realize this lesson when loved ones die, others learn this when acquaintances die. Sometimes we must go through the diagnosis and treatment of someone close to us who has a life-threatening illness. Perhaps we even experience this ourselves. A phenomenon that often occurs, to both the person involved and their family members, is that they begin to truly appreciate the gifts of life. They become the risk-takers they weren't before. They find new courage. They revel in simple pleasures, watching beautiful sunsets or storm clouds rolling in. As you observe them, you see their desire to fully live each moment. You don't see them fretting over plans gone awry or broken fingernails. They suddenly have no fear to say exactly what they are thinking or feeling, including expressions of love and passion. They have learned not to take anyone or anything for granted. They *flow through life* with a smile on their face, full of appreciation.

I often recommend a book for my clients that discusses what the authors call "mortality therapy." This therapy matches what I believe in examining our fears around death. In *Life is Uncertain, Eat Dessert First*, Sol Gordon and Harold Brecher offer us a dose of this therapy:

"We are all afflicted with a fatal illness called life. The only difference between most of us and those who have been given the bad news is we are less sure as to how much time we have left. Why wait until a medical diagnosis shocks you into adding more life to your days."

After you stop and ponder that last quote, you might want to ask yourself these questions: Why do I live with such limitations, fears and unhappiness, postponing doing what I truly desire? Why is risking change so threatening to me? Why do I deny myself pleasures that down deep I know I deserve? What is keeping me from saying "I love you" to those I love, or being more playful, or pushing myself less to accomplish more or be so perfect? Why do anxiety thoughts tend to dominate my mind?

This little gem of a book lists several methods of using mortality therapy to assist you in becoming unstuck from living marginally. Some of these processes include writing your own eulogy or will. If you decide to write your own eulogy, notice what was

64

important to you, what you think loved ones would say about you, how much joy versus how much pain you allowed into your life, how you chose to react to so-called negative circumstances. Then ask yourself if *this is how you are currently living.*

A good life is like a good play - it has to
have satisfying and exciting third act.

----- *Ethel Barrymore*

I frequently ask my clients to write themselves a letter that begins with the sentence, "If I had six months to live, this is what I would do, this is what I would truly value, this is how I would feel." Imagining that you only have a short time to live helps clarify your values and define priorities. To continue to examine our values throughout life, especially as we age and reach mid-life, is an important assessment process. We may have different values at 45 than we had at 25, and yet we may still be living our lives by the old standards. Perhaps we need to revise our game plan!

One little trick I try now and then is to pinch myself first thing in the morning to remind myself I am alive, then continue to pinch myself throughout the day when I find myself worrying, regretting something, feeling discouraged, dealing with rudeness, etc. The simple pinch is a reminder to redirect my thoughts away from the negative and into more positive, solution-oriented thoughts. It also reminds me to review my reactions, that I am free to choose a different response to circumstances.

By knowing what our values are and by living each and every day in sync with those values, the odds increase that we will respect and trust ourselves more. This improves not only our self-regard, but helps us maintain healthier relationships as well.

If we are not able to address the topic of our own mortality, it is difficult to heal fear issues. Fear of death is the basis of many of our anxieties, while also robbing us of serenity and joy. It causes us to live restrictive rather than expansive lives. Some folks worry about life after death. Perhaps it is more beneficial to focus on life after birth!

Life is not a journey to the grave
with the intention of arriving safely
in a pretty and well-preserved body,
but rather to skid in broadside,
thoroughly used up, totally worn
out, and loudly proclaiming – '
WOW!! What a Ride!'

----- Author Unknown

Tools for Navigating Through Your Fears

- Using the questions posed in this chapter, write a paragraph or more expressing your response to each of these provocative queries to grasp a bit of mortality therapy. The questions:

    o Why do you live with such limitations, fears and unhappiness, postponing what you truly desire?

    o Why is risking change so threatening?

    o Why do you deny yourself pleasures that down deep you know you deserve?

    o What is keeping you from saying "I love you" to those you love, or having more fun, or pushing yourself less to accomplish more or be so perfect?

    o Why do anxiety thoughts tend to dominate your mind?

- Finish at least one of the following assignments: (Take a deep breath, acknowledge any fear that arises, give yourself permission to feel it, then release it.)
    - Write your own eulogy or will.
    - Pinch yourself each morning to remind yourself that you are alive; then, pinch yourself during the day when you find yourself worrying, regretting something, feeling discouraged, dealing with rudeness, etc.
    - Write yourself a letter that begins with the sentence, "If I had six months to live, this is what I would do, this is what I would truly value, this is how I want to live my life," (this one is especially beneficial for workaholic, perfectionist-types).

CHAPTER TEN

A FLYSPECK WON'T BE NOTICED

What an interesting life I had. And
how I wish I had realized it sooner!
                                    ----- *Colette*

After returning home from taking a journey, particularly an introspective type, most travelers report having a fresh, different and usually broader perspective of life. Looking back, that summarizes what my risk-adventure adjusted within me. I expanded personally as my capacity to view everything with a new vision and a profound sense of importance changed. *Perspective shifts are great aids in overcoming fear.*

As an American, my outlook on the rest of the world is from a different vantage point than the local residents where I was traveling. I have not had the visual or the historical perspective of thousands of years of human existence readily available to me that they have. The U.S. is a large country that focuses primarily on its own news, so I had not been exposed to the same kinds of stories that I began hearing in Europe. As an American, my physical proximity to other cultures is limited, and I had not enlightened myself as to many other ways of living. Suddenly being exposed to cultural diversity, I was delighted when abroad to learn new ways of being. All of this contributed to my outlook shifting and the healing of my fears.

My perspective expanded further when I realized, as an American, I do not see or feel the sufferings of others around the world in the same way that other inhabitants on our planet do. Visiting with people throughout my travels was quite educational, because most spoke very openly and directly about their philosophies, as well as current happenings in the world. Watching European news broadcasts was also informative. By being open and receptive in my mind and heart to a broader view, my own fears lessened.

One of my most valued experiences of perspective during my travels was a visit to the Grotte Fomme du Gant near Les Ezies, France. This grotte, a 200-meter long cave, is concealed within a simple hillside that lovingly envelops prehistoric paintings telling tales of life from 15,000 years ago. On the walls of this tiny treasure house are drawings showing how humans lived, interacted, creatively expressed and drew inspiration from nature. They left us fantastic gifts to look upon, in total awe, many, many centuries later.

Perhaps the worth of any lifetime
is measured more in kindness than in
competency.

----- *Rachel Naomi Remen, M.D.*

Part of the awakening I experienced was from the interpretations provided to me by my English-speaking guide. Showing us various drawings of bison and deer, she pointed out details that have led experts to believe that these Cro-magnon people were actually much more advanced than once thought. They had the insight to draw the animals in movement and interacting, distinguishing between male and female. My favorite was a painting of two deer leaning down, facing each other with the female licking the male's forehead.

It is difficult for me to verbalize the depth of feeling I had standing amidst those damp cave walls, how I felt being within touching distance of the physical drawings left by our ancestors. I felt as though I was experiencing a delightful demonstration of perspective right before my very eyes! I had goose bumps. My attitude, my outlook was *instantly* modified from my, oh so little life. This life of petty worries in which I get caught up. Suddenly I was able to view a much larger panorama.

It was also one of those times when I was completely present in the moment. I savored each and every second of that walk. I wasn't worrying about or contemplating anything in my life but those drawings and the messages I was receiving. **That** is a gift. I was so grateful for the courage I had within me that had taken me to this point on my journey and pleased with myself for opening up to learn so much.

Even though I was not on a sightseeing trip, during my external-internal journey I visited numerous other monuments from life long ago. These included dozens of castles and cathedrals, Roman ruins and artifacts that almost become commonplace because of their prevalence. I felt the tales of battles, hardships and heroics everywhere and the energy that is sensed from thousands upon thousands of humans who have walked these paths. All this profoundly touched me today, as it gave me wisdom I needed to place my anxieties in proper perspective.

My daily encounters with the people in Europe also deeply affected me. Despite "modern progress," (evidenced by changes such as a MacDonald's Restaurant along the promenade on the French Riviera or desire for longer work weeks) many of these folks remain laid-back, easy-going and enjoy living a simple life. The reminders of things important are continually at their feet. I was gratefully reminded along with them during my journey as I stopped to view their ancient sites.

I had the realization that I and my entire
generation, my whole civilization, in fact,
are going to be one thin layer of sediment
in the side of a cliff someday. Yet precisely
because it makes a flyspeck of a difference
whether I write my essays or not, somehow
this frees me up to write, to follow the calling,

or do whatever I want, because there is no
failure. Or rather, failure is already assumed.
I'm going to die and be a million years dead,
and anyone who might possibly judge me for
my pursuits and mistakes will be a fossil right
next to mine in that cliffside.

----- *Gregg Levoy   (In response to spending*
time at a retreat in New Mexico)

Being a true romantic, one of my favorite stories is one I heard from an adorable Scottish tour guide at the Edinburgh Castle. During the tour, he recalled many tragic stories of Scots fighting for freedom in that small but feisty country.   He told a tale of 30 Scotsmen retaking the castle that had been seized by 300 English soldiers, all because of the love one Englishman had for his lady in the town. Because he couldn't endure being away from his love any longer, he carefully jumped the castle wall one night. The Scotsmen found him and convinced him to give away the secret passage to the castle. The Scotsmen used the information, reclaimed the Castle and history was changed because of the love between two people.

At this same castle, I was able to stand in the room where Mary Queen of Scots, the first queen of Scotland, gave birth to King James VI, the first Scottish King of England.   That woman did **not** have an easy life. Almost every husband or lover of hers was brutally murdered, some in front of her eyes, and her own life ended with her being hanged by her own cousin, Queen Elizabeth I. I like to think that she had pizzazz, lots of spunk, enormous courage and something to talk about in the locker room after the game. I like to believe that she knew that living life is much more than just being alive, or even trying to live a long life. It seems to me that she lived anything *but* a mediocre life.

Because I was born with the surname Stewart, I like to think of myself as her descendant. I may not be, but what really matters is that *all* of us have gifts that have been handed down through those who have lived before us. These are gifts such as bravery, wisdom, a sense of adventure, tenacity, self-sufficiency, enlightenment and overcoming adversity. These contributions provide **me** inspiration to find courage and gusto to do whatever I find difficult. Our self-imposed limitations are usually only mirages that have poofed out of nothingness in our heads. They are often images that we conjure up that tell us we don't have the strength, intelligence or courage to extricate ourselves from living marginal or unhappy lives.

I am completely convinced that the present abilities you think you possess are mere shadows of the strengths you actually do possess. Just think how rich and full your life would be if you only believed this conviction of mine!

Learning about courageous people like Mary Queen of Scots, hearing about a love story that changed the history of a nation, viewing ancient relics that reminded me of how short my life truly is and considering different opinions about current happenings around

74

the world all gave me wonderful perspective. As my perceptions expanded, I became more relaxed, worried less, let go of petty complaints and simply started living life in the present moment more often. What a treat!

If, day after day, you do the opposite of
what you desire, you say the opposite
of what you believe, you allow yourself
to be pushed and pulled where you do
not want to go. There is no impunity for
mocking authenticity in this manner. The
most exhausting thing in my life is being insincere.

----- *Anne Morrow Lindbergh*

Tools for Navigating Through Your Fears

- Name five happenings, stories or personal revelations that have occurred in the past year that have assisted you in gaining true perspective. (i.e. a friend being diagnosed with a serious illness)

- What kinds of thoughts did you have after learning about some of the above stories? Did you desire to change anything in your life after your revelations and how will you follow through with the changes? If not, what kinds of changes are you interested in making at this time?

- Being authentic (being congruent with your beliefs, thoughts, feelings and actions) is essential to well-being. List a few ways that you have allowed yourself to compromise your values or act in ways that are contrary to your genuine self, (i.e. participating in an activity with friends that you truly did not want to, or perhaps you believed it was not ethical).

CHAPTER ELEVEN

DELECTABLE BURNT MARSHMALLOWS

The most common despair is...not
choosing, or willing, to be oneself,
(but) the deepest form of despair
is to choose to be another than oneself.

----- *Soren Kierkegaard*

As we grow up in families that are less than perfect (and I assure you every family has its problems), we each learn to develop amazing coping strategies for survival that can be quite effective for many years. However, as we head into our 30's or 40's, many of these techniques or defenses no longer work for us. In fact, many become problematic, as the former coping strategies themselves can create new challenges. The sack that holds our baggage from the past reaches its maximum capacity, and as it bursts, unpleasant debris hits us in the face. This pain, however, does tend to motivate us (if we so choose) to look more closely at our lives and what we may need to change. In looking at defense mechanisms, I will say that they do serve a significant purpose in our lives, as being totally open, raw and vulnerable all at once does not often feel real great, nor does it always serve us well. The turtle has a shell for a reason!

The keys to examining and using our defenses to aid us:

1) Identify what they are
2) Recognize when they are flaring up
3) Learn to use them as warning signs to facilitate processing circumstances and relationship issues in our life.

When learning about our fears, it is helpful to gain knowledge of our defenses, as many anxieties are disguised as other behaviors. Our fears will remain and continue to haunt us until we acknowledge our defenses, or look beneath them. *Our defenses slyly conceal our fears.* It is similar to covering up a sinkhole in the ground with a blanket and expecting to be able to drive a car over it. Some of the popular defenses people use are:

rationalizing, laughter, intellectualizing, joking, analyzing, blaming, withdrawal, anger, silence and attacking; as well as compulsive behaviors such as: cleaning, computer overuse, frenetic behavior, sex, work, eating, religion, shopping, gambling and substances.

It's important to understand that these are not *bad* behaviors, we all need to eat and shop occasionally! It is how these behaviors are used, or misused, that needs to be examined.

Do not be too timid or squeamish about your actions. All life is an experiment.

----- *Ralph Waldo Emerson*

As I describe one of my favorite defenses by which I avoid feeling, perhaps you can look at how your own favorite defenses hide your feelings, specifically your fear. Mine is over-analyzing. Often when I fail to take needed action, I find that I am frequently over-thinking everything. As I continue sidestepping the real reason for stagnation – fear – it becomes difficult to expand. Keep in mind that we cannot change something if we don't recognize it is there. Much of the passion I feel in my heart, that fuel that helps thrust me forward in life, is often lost as I deny my emotions through over-thinking.

Being too intellectual when faced with a decision diminishes to a great extent that fuel I need to act. Enthusiasm energizes us. A small flame cannot be expected to ignite a huge rocket. The heat of excitement is necessary to boost us up. Thank goodness I have learned through life experiences to trust my gut, value my intuition and listen to my heart. But I still find that on many occasions I allow my head-talk, my rational and practical side, to talk my "knowing" out of what it knows. In the process of thinking, re-thinking and then adding more for good measure, I lose days and years staying stuck where I no longer wish to be. Next, I consult a few friends to add their thoughts to the mix. Then I wait until I think the perfect moment will arrive for a change. This is despite the fact that at this point in my life I KNOW there is no such *perfect* moment! Bottom line: As I spend my time over-analyzing, I dance around my fears instead of facing them straight on.

You gain strength, courage and confidence
by every experience in which you really
stop to look fear in the face. You are able
to say to yourself, 'I lived through this
horror. I can take the next thing that
comes along.' You must do the thing you
think you cannot do.

----- *Eleanor Roosevelt*

Besides intellectualizing, another common protective technique many people use is acting tough or stoic. A burnt marshmallow is a great metaphor to describe a few of these defenses. Burnt marshmallow people are still quite soft and delectable on the inside, but they have chosen to respond to the experiences of their life by forming a tough, crisp, darkened crust around their heart. Sadly, they mistakenly believe this will prevent them from being hurt again. What they don't realize is how the crustiness of the burned part does indeed push people away, but at the same time it barricades their own joy. Their perceived insensitive behavior, their toughness, is not viewed as a call for love. Nor is the *fear* recognizable that is often beneath the surface. Many of these burnt marshmallow people are simply trying to protect huge, tender hearts that they really have. They end up living their lives feeling alone, while the crustiness they use as a shield actually keeps their fears locked inside.

Our many defenses bear amazing variances of faces and personality types. Sadly, our perfected forms of defenses turn into fences. Some are barbed wire and some electric shock-types. Some are huge, thick cement walls. Do we think we are keeping people out, or do we realize that we are actually imprisoning ourselves? Numbing feelings, diminishing passion?

What is essential is to examine our heart, our emotions, and ask ourselves what we truly want and what stops us from going for it. What are we really afraid of? Part of that crusty exterior on the marshmallow is simply a reaction to heartache. A pretense of not really needing or wanting love. Love is the Core of our being. And as we use the knife called fear to cut ourselves off from that essence, from loving, we chop away the foundation that is life. *Our life.* One of my favorite quotes, from the wisdom of Simone Weil, describes what many of us do to sabotage ourselves: "The danger is not that the soul should doubt whether there is any bread, but that, by a lie, it should persuade itself that it is not hungry."

As we cut ourselves off from our feelings and desires, we often end up denying ourselves passion, as we tell ourselves lies about our mundane lives. We justify staying in mediocre, unfulfilling circumstances time and again. It is difficult for many of us to ignore our deep desires, however, as we review a book or movie such as *Bridges of Madison County.* Through an unfolding story that taps into a common mind-set of many women and men, author Robert James Waller accomplishes a remarkable feat by touching many hearts.

The story begins following the heroine's death, as her two adult children are going through their mother's memoirs. They read a letter she wrote for them that takes us back to the time of her short-lived, passionate love affair with a man they never knew. The story is ranked among many film buffs as one of the saddest movies of all times. Why? Because we watch the short four-day transformation of this middle-aged, bored and under-stimulated female evolve into a sparkling, glowing woman who feels passion and excitement about herself and someone else again. After those four days, she realizes how she has *lost herself* as she fulfills her duties to her husband and children. When I watched this movie for the first time, I was feeling trapped within an already-dead marriage. I wept profusely as she lay in the bathtub with her lover and later told her children, "I was acting like another woman, yet I was more myself than ever before." In the act of betraying her husband, she was struck by the realization that she had been betraying herself for many years. I easily recognized the pain she felt as I realized I too had sold myself short. I had lost my true self along the way. My heartrending, unexpected reaction to this film was motivation to begin re-thinking how I had relinquished being responsible for my own well-being.

We must be willing to get rid of the life
we've planned, so as to have the life that
is waiting for us.

----- *Joseph Campbell*

Another angle to view when examining our defenses or façades is to look at how we ultimately sell ourselves short by being unauthentic. We often keep up images that are not congruent with who we genuinely are in an effort to please other people. "To thine own self be true." (William Shakespeare) As my heroine Maude reminds us, "Everyone has a right to make an ass of themselves. You just can't let the world judge you too harshly." Over the course of your lifetime, how much time and energy do you suspect you have spent trying to make sure people like you, approve of you and your actions? It would probably be fairly over-whelming if we could take that one trait of ourselves, make a video of our entire life emphasizing that component and watch how much energy we've spent worrying about what others think of us. I'm sure if I sat and watched mine, I would cringe in agony!

How much of this people pleasing do you suppose stems from fear? Fear of not being good enough, of not doing the "right" thing, of making mistakes or appearing foolish. The more confidence I have in being my authentic self, in honoring who and what I am, and living from that genuine place, the less fear I have. Especially less anxiety about what others will think.

Early in my career I began noticing how much distress people experience as adults still trying to win the approval of their parents, in-laws or significant others. It's a very common theme. Many adults are still fearful of living their lives as they would really like. They are still not sure who *they* are and are often unable to stand their ground or express what they feel or want or need. This approval seeking may even continue after the parents are no longer living. Because of having lived as their parents, or other authority figures, designed them, many are still not positive of their own identity. They are afraid to step outside the box they are in. The desire to feel parental approval frequently transfers to a spouse, children or even a boss, as they end up molding themselves into the person others think they should be. *They lose themselves among the high expectations of others.* I'm not suggesting you do not act considerately with those you love or listen to their viewpoints, only that your behavior genuinely reflects who **you** are and that your choices are made with no ulterior motives or agendas.

No (woman) was ever ruined from without;
the final ruin comes from within.

----- *Amelia E. Barr*

Tools for Navigating Through Your Fears

- Many behaviors we exhibit are actually defenses to supposedly protect us from what we perceive to be threatening or fearful possibilities. Using some of those listed in this chapter (or others you recognize in yourself), write about each of your favorite defenses and be sure to include specific examples of their use in your daily life, (i.e. working over-time to avoid an intimate relationship that needs attention).

- Are some of your defenses making you look and feel like a burnt marshmallow? If so, list how you use toughness or stoic behaviors in an attempt to keep from getting hurt.

- Can you think of any ways you have betrayed yourself, or sold yourself short, in order to please another? (Note: Be careful with all of these assignments not to drop into self-loathing thoughts about your actions. You are simply trying to identify these self-defeating behaviors so that you can recognize them. The next time you find yourself preoccupied with self-defeating thoughts, say "Oops, I've done it again!" Simply stop yourself and move into a more constructive response.)

CHAPTER TWELVE

GOING WITH THE FLOW

Doubt may be an uncomfortable condition, but certainty is a ridiculous one.

----- *Voltaire*

Learning to *enjoy living in the present moment* is one of the most difficult and most important life skills to learn. Many of us have heard this philosophy. Most of us probably believe it is true. Living it is not so easy.

Following the terrorist attacks on September 11, a sickness began dominating our normally spunky American attitude, which I now label "Projection Maladjustment Illness." As a society, we have contaminated each other with this fear-based sickness, and in the process we have lost sight of living in the present moment. Instead, many have begun to obsess about "what if's." Others have had such anxiety that at times their ability to enjoy the present moment is obliterated.

Projecting into the future in connection with negative thoughts is a sure recipe for squelching joy in the present moment.

Not living in the present moment not only wreaks havoc on our clear thinking and interferes with our ability to make sound choices, it also acts as a firefighter's hose dousing the fire of life within us. It easily snuffs out our spark.

As our collective consciousness fuels more fear, (i.e. watching the news) it begins to show up in our homes and individual lives. I have seen hundreds of people sabotage their own happiness through excessive worry, or through attempting to control a situation. Projected fear is often used as a powerful weapon with which people manipulate others, and it can become a pawn in relationship games that people play. When a significant person in our life is pushing our fear button, it is usually difficult to maintain composure. Their tendency to do this is frequently a by-product of the button pushers not having dealt with their own fears. They may not have a clue that their own fear is at the base of their attempts to project that fear onto their loved one. When we carry around that unrecognized fear, it surfaces easily and reaches out to infect others. Sometimes it infiltrates entire family systems. When we remain preoccupied in an anxious state regarding relationship issues, particularly if fear is the foundation of the issues, today's joy certainly slips away.

If Joan of Arc could turn the tide of an entire war before her eighteenth birthday, you can get out of bed.

----- *D. Jean Carroll*

Learning to live in the present moment is probably one of the most valuable and concrete behavioral changes I made during my trip to Europe. When I shared this revelation with friends upon my return home, their common reaction was, "Sure, it was easy for you without your daily obligations and worries." Granted, I was not under my usual time constraints. BUT (and this is important so I hope you're paying attention) the daily details were always just my *excuse*. My excuse for not being fully present to what is delightfully happening **right now**.

As we navigate through fear, it is helpful to examine the issue of accepting responsibility for our choices. Self-empowering choices that we make each instant of each hour of every day. Self empowerment reduces anxiety. As my journey in Europe continued, I began to reflect on how choices I have made (thoughts, words and actions) have often kept me from living in the present moment. I have used numerous distractions to justify stagnation and to hide my fears. *It is important to admit that I have always done this to myself.* It is not about the specific circumstance du jour that keeps me from truly enjoying the day at hand. It's always *my* choice regarding my response to these circumstances that is essential.

We have all been given the freedom to choose our thoughts. To catch them as they spiral downhill is not an easy task! Is freedom a curse or a gift? You decide. At times it is extremely difficult not to project into the future or to live in the past. Learning to go with the flow helps us meet each day with an attitude of enjoying the mystery in every moment. I learned to flow much more easily as I continued on my journey, and as I did I was able to simply enjoy the moment at hand.

Try not to try too hard, it's just a lovely ride.

----- *James Taylor*

From "The Secret of Life"

There is a story of one such place along my journey that illustrates how this happened for me. I had just spent three wonderful days in one of my favorite places in the world, the Dordogne River Valley in southwest France. Through its beauty, tranquility and historic castles, this region offered me peace and contentment. I was able to experience the serenity of the life enjoyed by others before me as I walked quietly along picturesque country roads. I made a conscious choice to be in a very peaceful state of mind. Instead of focusing on a complaining knee for *many* more miles than I originally anticipated, my very hungry stomach and other such "negatives," I decided to focus my mind entirely on the gifts right before me, savoring each of the treasures and joys that were so evident. These riches appeared because I consciously chose to see them. *I allowed myself the pleasure* of experiencing them. Looking back now, I do not know if that particular place was so magical or if it was just my view of it.

I left the Dordogne one lovely autumn morning and headed to the home of a spunky, lively 78 year-old lady named Leone, the mother of a friend of mine. Living with her was her 55 year-old turtle, Caroline. I was going to spend a few days with both of those wise females in the southwest part of France. Normally this trip would take about two hours by car, but as I soon learned, going with the flow sometimes requires throwing out the clock. For me, the first segment of the journey was by bus.

I have found that many French bus drivers are adventurous types who love the challenge of squeezing through tight spots along the road, and they certainly don't allow other vehicles to intimidate them into budging one inch. As we sped through the winding countryside, I decided to take singer/songwriter James Taylor's advice and simply enjoy the ride. I did **not** feel a need to "help the driver out" by watching the road, wondering if he was speeding, why we were weaving or if he was doing his job just right! We seemed to brush the sides of ancient homes and storefronts as we whizzed through small villages. Instead, I was able to let go and enjoy the journey. I thoroughly soaked up every detail of the gorgeous valley and historic sites. I hope to return to the Dordogne some day, but because life is uncertain and doesn't always go as planned, I simply relaxed and immersed myself in the pleasure of the moment. I absorbed as much as possible during that 45-minute bus ride.

True beauty in a woman is reflected in her soul. It is the caring that she lovingly gives, the passion that she shows. And the beauty of a woman only grows with passing time.

----- *Audrey Hepburn*

The next leg of my journey to Leone and Caroline's home was a two-hour layover at a small train station, set at the edge of a petite village. I discovered that the station was a long distance from the town and anything to see or do. As I awaited my train, I looked forward to spending a quiet two hours in the sun, reading and writing in my journal. That I did. It was marvelous. During my wait, the schedule announcing the arrival of my train changed approximately every 30 minutes or so, with each increment prolonging the arrival of my train from Paris. Because of the normally punctual European train system, I was surprised when the train ended up being about eight hours late. The delay presented me with unexpected gifts of meeting and visiting with delightful French people I would otherwise not have had the opportunity to get to know.

One of my favorite Frenchmen was Maurice, an 83 year-old airplane pilot from days gone by and now an art dealer in Toulouse. He barely spoke English, but we still managed to communicate! I was fascinated with his language. I spent hours listening intently to his tales, life lessons, stories of love and passions. Through the sparkle in his eyes and his broad smile, he allowed me into his heart and revealed how his seemingly ordinary life had been lived in a most extraordinary way. As he spoke of his life adventures, I did not sense any fear in him. He was kind, polite and considerate to me all the way until I exited the train that we rode together, twelve hours after my trip had begun. He insisted on walking with me to the train door and helping with my bag. All this despite his difficulty walking on solid ground, let alone managing the sway of the train car.

Reflecting back over the course of the day, I realized how much I enjoyed the way several of us bonded throughout our delay. Many schedules had been disrupted, but *no one* seemed very disgruntled. I was amazed, since I've noticed considerable frustration over similar situations traveling in the U.S. I didn't hear any blaming or complaining about the situation. Nor did I observe any rude behavior toward the station employees. (By the way, the employees were most congenial and offered us whatever assistance we needed.) As I finally lay warmly tucked in Leone's spare bed that night, I promised myself I would remember the gifts of that day. I would attempt to live by those lessons as I return to my driven and hectic American lifestyle.

As I enjoyed living in the moment, I had practiced simply going with the flow.

My serenity continued as I spent the next three days with Leone and Caroline, staying focused on the moment at hand. We communicated beyond the language differences, as Leone taught me a great deal about French culture and life in general in a very short time. We connected in a magical way. The evening before I left, Caroline went into hibernation for the winter. Leone died exactly two months later. When I heard that news, I was more than ever grateful that I had the opportunity to share a bit of life with this spirited and wise woman. I was especially glad I had savored each moment of those precious days with her.

You must take your chance.

----- *William Shakespeare*

Tools for Navigating Through Your Fears

- Which is your most popular pattern of avoiding living in the present moment – over-focus on the past or projecting, worrying about the future? (If you are one who is skilled at living totally in the NOW, congratulations and keep it up!)

- How does this show up in your life, i.e. what specific thoughts continue to circle around your mind keeping you in the past or future?

- Try to identify what "pay-offs" you get, how you benefit, from the thoughts that keep you in the past or future? (What do these thoughts keep you from enjoying today?)

- Think about your reaction in the months following 9/11, and ask yourself if you have become more fearful in general about situations in the world or in your own life. If so, how can you begin to let go of this needless anxiety and get back to living more joyfully in the present?

CHAPTER THIRTEEN

FLOWING WITH THE GO

*We cannot become what we need
to be, by remaining who we are.*

----- *Oprah Winfrey*

This phenomenon of people enjoying the company of other people happened on another occasion along my journey. This time three days before I left for home. It was a different train station and the delay was only about three hours that evening, but the camaraderie was similar to the first story. People took me under their wings like mother ducks do their ducklings in a storm. Instead of griping about the inconveniences we were experiencing, we shared food, laughter and stories. Though friends were waiting for me in a city about 90 minutes away to attend a large French/American Thanksgiving celebration, I chose not to fret about circumstances over which I had no control. In fact, each *moment* at that train station was a celebration to me! It may have been cold and rainy outside, but it was bright and warm in the hearts of all those who waited that evening.

During both delays, I lived in the moment, gave people my undivided attention and they gave me theirs. What better gift is there to give and receive? We made each other smile. One young man was wearing a Denver Avalanche hockey team hat and was delighted to find out I was from Colorado and could discuss the team. Claudine, who spoke not one word of English, eventually told me with tears and sadness that both her husband and son had died within the past year. I felt privileged that she shared intimately and trusted me so after meeting just a few hours earlier. We touched each other's lives in special, yet ordinary, ways.

I don't believe any of this would have happened if I had not been determined to live in the present moment and to go with the flow. I allowed myself the FULL adventure of living. I met each moment as it arrived. I delighted in giving and receiving, rather than fretting over the delays or the inconvenience. I didn't worry about what would happen next. It was interesting how smoothly events unfolded as I relaxed and let go of any projected fear.

It's a funny thing about life. If you refuse to settle for anything less than the best, that's what it will give you.

----- W. Somerset Maugham

Despite what we perceive as negative happenings, being fully awake to the present moment invites rapture and joy. Eleanor Roosevelt once said, "Life has got to be lived--that's all there is to it. At 70 I would say the advantage is that you take life more calmly. You know that, 'This too, shall pass.'" When we follow her advice and go with the flow, each event in life becomes more delightful.

How the time flew by on my journey. The perception of time is such a fascinating subject that it could fill an entire book by itself. Have you ever noticed when you are engrossed in a project, let's say a hobby that you love, you look up after hours of working and are amazed by the time that has flown by. It's because you were living fully and joyfully in the NOW. You were absorbed in what you were doing rather than recalling the past or projecting into the future. Ideally this is how every instant should be lived. But, sadly what we tend to do instead is to "be" somewhere else rather than soaking up the moment at hand.

There will never be a better time or more opportunity to experience joy, completeness, prosperity, love, success, fulfillment or whatever you are wanting than this present moment.

Don't misunderstand the point. I am not trying to say that I believe we should just resign ourselves to what is dished out to us. Living in the now does not mean you do not have dreams or goals. That you should accept your present limitations. This isn't about living a marginal life and being satisfied with less than absolute good, whatever your view of good may be. It is about living a full, rich life as you delightfully go through it one moment at a time.

Discontent and disorder (are) signs
of energy and hope, not despair.
----- *Dame Cicely Veronica Wedgewood*

Learning to live in the present moment means releasing the past. I tend to romanticize the past and remember it through the eyes of a fairytale-type mentality, which sometimes distorts its reality. I want to learn the valuable from all that I've experienced and use that knowledge to expand my awareness of my True Self. I want my past to teach me what I want and need *in the present.*

Because of a belief system that told me the past was better, I have robbed myself of many beautiful present moments. Or, at times I allow the pain of my former life to continue to control my life today. A painful incident from the past is completed, like spent energy or money. It's over now. I already allowed that situation to rob me of happiness at the time it happened! Why would I want to allow someone or some event that caused me pain in the past to continue to drain me of the joy of today? If I remain focused on a past circum-stance about which I feel resentful, I slowly diminish my own power and give that power away. It feels just like heat going out in the cold through an open door.

As we carry around resentments, they often turn to fear. This fear can keep us from risking and enjoying the pleasures of the present moment. Many people cling to love wounds from the past that rob them of love today. What a rip-off! It reminds me of a runner who carries a very heavy, uncomfortable sack on her back, full of races not won or times when she stumbled and fell. This bag of previous painful memories prevents her from participating in and loving the race before her today. This lesson involves not only releasing others or past events, but *your* former self as well. Growth and learning from the past cannot happen if we cling to it.

Life is lived forward, but understood backward.

----- *Soren Kierkegaard*

Worrying about the future is the other side of the fear coin. It prevents us from enjoying the only time we truly have. *Now.* If we constantly think tomorrow will bring us happiness, we are living in the illusion that the future will fix all our problems. Fretting about taking that new job, committing to that new love relationship or moving to that new place, we stagnate in the mire of today's waters. Guess what? There **is** no tomorrow. When it gets here, it's another today.

This does not mean you shouldn't dream or plan or risk. We all have talents that we fail to recognize. If we are granted a vision about sharing our gifts with the world, it is an assignment that is coming *through us.* Our task is to accept the opportunities to give these contributions away. The means to accomplish this, the ability to stay on the right track is also given to us *if* we are open and willing to listen. The green light indicating we're on the right track becomes clear as we relax, live in the present moment and tune into Divine Guidance. Our job is to empty that blasted backpack of trash from the past and worry about the future so we can prepare ourselves for today's gifts.

The following story, sent to me by a dear friend, contains a beautiful lesson within it.

There once was a king who had offered a prize to the artist who would paint the most beautiful painting representing peace. Many tried. The king looked at all the paintings, but liked only two of them, and he had to choose between the two.

The first one represented a calm lake, a perfect mirror, surrounded by high mountains. The sky was blue with white, woolly clouds. All those who saw that painting thought is was a perfect representation of peace.

The other one also had mountains, but they were sheer and rocky. The sky above them was dark, full of rain and lightening. Near the mountain, a foamy waterfall. It was in no way a picture of peace. But when the king looked at it, he saw behind the waterfall a very small shrub that was growing in a crevice. In the shrub, a mother bird had built her nest...perfect peace.

The king chose the second picture: "Because," he explained, "peace doesn't mean being in a place where there is no noise, no problem, no hardship. Peace means being in the middle of all these things, and yet being calm within your heart."

Trust yourself. Create the kind of self that you will be happy to live with the rest of your life. Make the most of yourself by fanning the tiny sparks of possibility into flames of achievement. Dare to be different. Set your own pace. You are more than flesh and blood...you are a god discovering her own living potential.

----- Author Unknown
(I read this somewhere about 30 years ago, memorized it and have used it to direct much of my life)

Tools for Navigating Through Your Fears

- What activity, hobby, or project that you become absorbed in makes time fly by for you?

- What is it about this activity that causes you to lose yourself in it?

- Name one relationship or event in your past that you believe still controls your life to some degree today? (i.e. anger or hurt you experienced over a job or relationship loss) Are you ready to release your attachment to this?

- Remember the fear list you compiled following Chapter 2? Get it out and divide the list into two columns –

  a) those which you can do something about and

  b) those over which you have no control and can release. Once you complete the "a" list, write a brief statement describing what steps you can take to resolve the fears you listed, and be sure to name a time limit for their release. What would you like to do with the "b" list? How will you do that? Save this entire assignment, as you will need it later.

CHAPTER FOURTEEN

UNFOLDING LIKE AN EXQUISITE FLOWER

Sail on silver girl. Sail on by.
Your time has come to shine,
all your dreams are on their way.

----- *Paul Simon*
From "Bridge Over Troubled Waters"

The Rainbow Story: Just before embarking on my journey, I received a profound message. It reignited my desire to change my life and reinforced my need to let go of the way I had been living. It happened the last day I counseled clients in my private practice in the small mountain community where I had lived for nearly 20 years. I was feeling fear and trepidation about giving up my well-worn career and the perceived security that I believed it provided. Also sadness from saying good-bye to people I cared about. My grief included bidding farewell to this region of Colorado that had brought me great joy and peace. Once again I experienced the familiar tug between leaving and staying that this lovely town evokes. It envelops its inhabitants as a soft, warm blanket gives security to newborn babies. It seemed to pacify me somehow for many years, while it had also restrained me for too long a time. Letting go is difficult, especially if the next step is not so certain.

As I drove away through puddles of water from my office, I noticed the familiar mountain weather phenomenon of rain and sunshine at the same time. I smiled softly, knowing there was a rainbow somewhere nearby. Over the years I had delighted in viewing many of these splendid wonders. As I headed east through town and on to the highway, lo and behold, there *it* was. Right in front of me. I drove on automatic pilot for the next ten minutes, aware of nothing but the glistening, vibrant colors that decorated the sky. With each foot I traveled, the rainbow became larger and more distinct, clear and bright as a perfect palette of paints. It was so spectacular that I thought perhaps for a moment I had died and hadn't realized it!

As I began crossing the land bridge over the lake, this magnificent rainbow came down to earth and began to touch me! One end of the rainbow was directly on the right side of the hood of my car and the other end on the left side. I had every color in my sight at all times. *It totally enfolded me.*

Birds sing hopeful songs on dismal days,
They've learned to live life as they should,
They are at peace with nature's ways.

----- *Don McLean*
From " Winterwood"

I have never had a visual occurrence strike me so clearly as a sign from God as that one did. My friends and I have often joked about wanting to hear God's message come down from the heavens in a loud, booming voice giving us clear direction. And there it was! Except it wasn't an audible voice. At that moment it was completely apparent that this was a beautiful gift. One of the best I have ever received.

The message I received: "You are doing the right thing, leaving the old and moving on to the new. Don't be afraid, because my Peace, Strength and Wisdom will be with you all the way."

I felt a complete and indescribable serenity. I didn't want that moment to end but I knew it would (unless I had indeed died!), so I savored each second of that gift. Tears of joy were pouring down my face. There was a *knowing* that I felt deep within me, reassuring me that all was well. I felt overwhelming gratitude for the Source of my being.

Using nature to help us learn and heal is an incredibly powerful tool available to all, *if* we open our heart to its powers. The subject of eco-psychology has increased awareness in recent years of how nature can truly restore people to health, physically and emotionally. Eco-psychology's basic premise is that by allowing nature to nurture and heal us, we become healthier and wiser and in turn will naturally take better care of Mother Nature's gifts.

There are many books on the subject, and one of my favorite authors is a very kind and conscientious man, Howard Clinebell. One assignment he suggests is to re-explore and write about experiences we had as a child when we were out in nature. He asks us to remember those times we loved playing outdoors, recalling how nurturing they were at that moment.

Having been raised in Kansas and Wisconsin, I spent many hours outside building tree or snow forts, playing in or near streams and woods, as well as visiting the farms of aunts, uncles and grandparents. Completing Clinebell's assignment was easy and fun for me. It was a joy traveling back in time, smelling the dampness of many seasons' bounty of leaves in the Wisconsin woods. Hearing the trickle of melting snow along the walk home from school as my brother and I gleefully sloshed through the slush. I remembered my awe watching my grandfather dig up potatoes and carrots in his garden. For the first time, I realized that they don't grow packaged in plastic wrap for the grocery store!

Give your dreams all you've got,
and you'll be amazed at the energy
that comes out of you.

----- *William James*

As an adult, I chose to live and raise my two children in one of the most beautiful places on earth, the Colorado Rockies. I knew I needed a "nature fix" on a regular basis and believed my kids would too. As adults who have at times moved away, both of my children have told me what they miss most about living in the mountains are the clear, beautiful stars twinkling brightly through pitch black skies.

During the times of my life when I've wrestled with important decisions, or when I've struggled through a stressful or traumatic event, nature has been one of the most soothing tonics I have found. One of the gifts it offers, as I have said, is perspective. And perspective is a remarkable aid for navigating through fear.

At the end of the film *Grand Canyon*, Danny Glover has taken Kevin Klein and his family out of the city life of Los Angeles to stand at the edge of the Grand Canyon in Arizona. He is giving them the gift of perspective as they contrast their petty worries and trials of life to the immensity of this natural wonder. Glover tells his friends, "The rocks are laughing at us." And it's true! We are barely a speck in the big picture compared to the billions of years they've been here, and our fears certainly fade within the vast expanse of geologic time.

Live in the sunshine, swim the sea, drink the wild air's salubrity.

----- *Ralph Waldo Emerson*

After seeing that movie, I began looking for smiling faces in the rocks where I lived, especially as I drove through the canyons that lead to Estes Park. *It's amazing what we can find once we begin looking for something.* I have discovered delightful, happy faces grinning at me as I go about my travels. I have even taken photos of a few and keep them out where I can see them daily, just to remind me to lighten up when I need to. If you listen intently, I'll bet you can hear rocks laughing too, cheerfully reminding you to put your problems in perspective!

All along my journey in Europe when I became bothered, afraid or lonely, I used gifts from Mother Earth to nurture me and bring me comfort. The soothing flow of slow, rambling rivers throughout France and Germany brought me peace. I often use rivers as a means to discard concerns and worries, "dumping" my perceived troubles in the water and letting them gently flow away. Then when I look upstream from the bank, I allow the power and strength of the water to fill me with life, energy and hope.

Eastern philosophies have believed for centuries that water is the most amazing element there is because it is non-resistive, yet so incredibly powerful. We can all learn from it as we watch its patterns of allowing, simply flowing. It doesn't resist the rocks, curves or detours along its path. It simply flows around or over its apparent obstacle, continuing on its merry way, babbling a happy tune as it goes. Eventually, without attacking, fretting or fleeing, the peaceful substance wears down rocks and even constructs canyons with its force.

James Dillet Freeman, an inspiring, loving man and poet extraordinaire, wrote a poem that reminds us how marvelous rivers truly are. I suggest you read it and then read it again to absorb his beautiful message into your heart and life:

"Rivers hardly ever run in a straight line.
Rivers are willing to take ten thousand meanders
And enjoy every one, And grow from every one --
When they leave a meander, they are always more
Than when they entered it.
When rivers meet an obstacle,
They do not try to run over it;
They merely go around –
But they always get to the other side.
Rivers accept things as they are,
Conform to the shape they find the world in –
Yet nothing changes things more than rivers;
Rivers move even mountains into the sea.
Rivers hardly ever are in a hurry –
Yet is there anything more likely
To reach the point it sets out for
Than a river?

Tools for Navigating Through Your Fears

- Write one entire page (use extra paper) about your childhood experiences, focusing especially on the times you played outdoors, fun times with your friends and family, or even lessons you learned in school about nature in one form or another. Try to recall specific sights, sounds and smells. (People reared in cities may have visited zoos or parks, enjoyed household pets, watched T.V. or movies showing the beauty and joys of nature, or taken vacations for the pleasure of appreciating natural wonders.)

- How do you use nature today to nurture yourself? What are some ways you can begin to utilize these gifts more regularly?

- What is one thing you can do *this* month to thank Mother Nature for her gifts by assisting with the preservation of her resources?

CHAPTER FIFTEEN

WHEN THE FLOWER OPENS, THE BEES WILL COME

I watch the night cover the landscape.
Then, looking up at the stars, I steep
myself in the insignificance of earthly
things....Then I feel a secret solace
passing through me.

----- Charles de Gaulle

One day on my journey along the Mediterranean coast in Nice, France, I again was transported into a dream by nature. It was an unusually stormy day, with constant torrential rain that is uncommon in autumn. I had spent the morning exploring the beautiful city, enjoying each slushy step despite drenched shoes and cold, soaked slacks. When I finally approached the oceanfront, I noticed that the road running along the coast was blocked off. I assumed there had been an accident. Then I noticed rapt, cautious on-lookers walking a safe distance from the beach along the famous

Cote d'Azur Promenade, the pedestrian walkway. Once I saw the sea, I was as awestruck as everyone else!

The ocean seemed very, very angry. The gigantic, brown waves rolled in such a strange manner that they appeared to be *alive*. The power that was generated by their strength was an unbelievable phenomenon. Severely immobilized and frozen in my place, I watched the movement of that water repeatedly approach the normally smooth pedestrian path. Sand and rocks had washed up onto the Promenade and roadway. I was both fascinated and frightened. Police along the walk kept curious tourists and locals from getting too close, and when I asked two of them if the ocean being this wild was a common occurrence, they answered with wide-opened eyes, "It has NEVER happened like this before."

Suddenly I felt an odd sense of detachment from myself and my surroundings, yet I remained intrigued. The reoccurring thought that struck me was *"This just doesn't seem real."* I felt like I was watching a computer-animated movie, something alive, but somehow artificial. I recalled Richard Bach describing in his book, *Illusions,* how our lives are only films projected up on a screen and we are the creators. Our imaginations are the projectors. Suddenly all of life – my life and everything I'd ever known – truly felt like an illusion, a dream.

Earth laughs in flowers.

----- *Ralph Waldo Emerson*

The sea spoke to me through the roar of the waves and a rumbling that vibrated through my entire being. It reminded me of how powerful, strong and uncontrollable nature is, all of life really. It was an unseen force that appeared in the ocean that day, just as beautifully as it had in the Colorado rainbow. I was reminded of what I truly am, *one part of a Greater Whole*. Just as I had received wisdom looking at the prehistoric cave drawings weeks earlier, the ocean gave me insight that washed away all my petty, insignificant concerns. In the blink of an eye, the sand had been whisked away. So had my fears. Somehow I felt the Power that moved those massive waves fill *me* up, and suddenly I felt totally unafraid. I felt invincible.

A few nights later I peacefully strolled along that same Promenade, keenly aware of the contrastingly calm water. As I gazed up at the full moon and beautiful stars shining down on the Mediterranean, I felt their unbelievable splendor reflecting within me. What extraordinary gifts Mother Nature bestows on us! No matter where I was along my journey, I felt reassured seeing the same moon and stars that I enjoy at home. In the same way I experienced peace on that first night flying across the Atlantic, I continued all along my path to feel the constant evidence of well-being that night skies provide.

Toward the end of the week, a new-found friend invited me to join him at the beach just before dawn to share a treat almost too sensational for words. Together, in silence, we beheld a most

116

magnificent sunrise over the Mediterranean! (see front cover) The beauty and power of that experience were unimaginable. Just when I thought it was as brilliant and golden as it could be, it gently rose another few inches and lit up the sky and water below with even more fervor and excitement. It seemed to say, "Wait! There's more! It gets even better. Don't give up yet!" I drank up every instant of that event and will keep it within me forever.

> *When the flower opens, the bees*
> *will come.*
>
> ----- *Kabir*

My mom always told me that the best things in life are free. I certainly believe her. Nature blesses us with thrills that money can't buy. Sadly, however, our extravagant lifestyles are taking their serious toll on these natural gifts that we have been so fortunate to take pleasure in. If we listen to the eco-psychologists and begin living healthier lives through learning from nature's treasure house of lessons, it seems logical that we would naturally want to do what we can to *sustain* our planet. Simple, natural beauty warms our hearts and enriches our lives. Her delightful surprises make us feel life is worthwhile.

Always tied to fear is our own self-respect, or lack of it. When we care for our environment, we are showing respect for everything and everyone on this planet, including ourselves. When we neglect what is at the core of our being, that which brings us insight and tranquility, our sense of self erodes. This inevitably impacts our response to events that we label fearful.

One bright, brisk day while in a petite village in France, I sat at an outdoor café enjoying some chocolate and banana crepes when I spotted a beautiful black and white tuxedo cat and her babies. She looked exactly like my beloved cat, Zippy. Since I was the only person eating outside, the happy family of cats decided to come closer in hopes of sharing some of my treats. I realized how tranquil I became as I watched and interacted with them for about an hour. Part of nature's gifts, and some of the greatest teachers we have, are creatures in the wild, or our own household pets.

Zippy was so much more than a "pet" to my children and me, for we all felt (as did he) that he was a member of our family. Animals have a guidance system (scientists call it instinct) that directs and enlightens them so that they not only survive, but take pleasure in living life with ease. That is one of the best messages they teach – how to simply *enjoy*! And how to enjoy living simply. We found Zippy in a box marked "free" by our local post office when he was five weeks old, took him home and he soon became the most wonderful freebie we ever received. Throughout his almost 18 years, he was gentle, affectionate, playful, easy-going, loved sleeping in the sun, being outdoors and smelling fresh air and all 16 pounds of him loved to eat. Those traits should teach us something!

118

The earth and myself are of one mind.

----- Thunder Rolling Down the Mountain
Popularly known as Chief Joseph, Peace
Advocate for the Nez Perce Tribe

The greatest lesson I learned from Zippy was to *go with the flow*...a way of living known by all creatures. Except humans. What do we do instead? Fret, worry and try to control everything. Or we regret, dwell on the past and spend enormous energy anticipating and manipulating the future. Zippy never seemed to blame or feel guilty. He rarely complained about anything, only an occasional screech when someone stepped on his tail. He was a very social cat who loved visitors and family. He helped me see the value in belonging and allowing myself to play with others. He found incredible joy in simple pleasures, such as hiding in boxes and wrapping paper at Christmas. He could amuse himself for hours playing with what we called Tinkerbell's light, or the sun's reflection on a moving object. Simple entertainment. He innately knew when people were upset and would come close and sit by them to be petted.

Zippy also taught me that giving is receiving, as the love I gave him always returned to me. He loved us all unconditionally, never suggesting that he would love us less if we weren't wealthy, good looking, intelligent or successful. He simply loved us. At night I loved cuddling with him under the covers, Zippy purring wildly all the while. Soothing both of us, his purrs of contentment became my

119

pleasure as well. His spirit was pure, honest and loving. I treasure his gifts. I would love to say I always maintain those same qualities that Zippy had, but sadly I too often stray from them. Mostly, I fail to love myself as unconditionally as he did.

It is always sunrise somewhere.

----- *John Muir*

Tools for Navigating Through Your Fears

- Find some source of water in your area (a river, lake, pond, ocean, waterfall in a hotel lobby or buy yourself a small bubbling fountain) and spend time observing and listening to this water. If possible, imagine throwing your "troubles and worries" into the water and picture them floating away. Next time you find them popping into your head, remind yourself that they have floated downstream.

- Recall a time when you had a favorite pet (or have now) and write down what this friend gave (gives) you and what you learned from her/him. Did you receive and give unconditional love? What does that do for you?

CHAPTER SIXTEEN

FOLLOWING SPIRIT'S COMPASS

Sometimes we find ourselves in a comfort-able situation, and we remain in it while a part of us dies. We become less prone to take a chance. Our need for security puts to death the boldness that is natural to the soul.

----- *Rev. Jim Rosemergy*

Have you ever watched how flocks of birds or schools of fish move together in perfect synchronization in a dance that is indescribably magical? Their movement is spontaneous as they all simultaneously respond to some Guidance that seems to whisper to them. Their turns happen in milliseconds of an instant and without them bumping into each other! They simply *know* -- how and where and when. I'm convinced that if we each listened as carefully to our own inner Guidance, we'd float through life as easily and merrily. Fear would fly away.

During my visit with friends in Germany, I was introduced to two of their companions who are not only magnificent musicians, but extraordinary human beings as well. Both are now dedicated to healing people holistically and spiritually through their music. One evening we all sat around a make-shift table in a tiny, rustic cabin we'd been remodeling all day, and as we savored in-depth communication and delicious German bread and wine, we pondered this question: If every living thing on this planet is ONE, what is the Greater Intelligence that connects all and how can we tap into that Power?

I had been studying the concept of Oneness for many years through *A Course in Miracles* classes. My friends in Germany had never read the *Course,* although they had heard about it somewhere. Initially, I was amazed how similar our studies and beliefs were without having any of the same teachers or books. It has become apparent to me, however, that this idea is now a universal trend, an inspiration whose time has come.

Every forest branch moves differently
in the breeze, but as they sway they
connect at the roots.

----- *Rumi*

Oneness. No separation, no separate minds, no separate bodies -- all hearts beating as one. All of life touching. When we hurt others, we hurt ourselves. When we love others, we are loving ourselves. And when we love ourselves, we are loving all. As my friends and I spoke about the fish and birds having this Higher Radar, or Spirit's Compass, we all agreed that this universal principle excludes no one, no animals, no humans. *Humans simply tune out this gift*, so it becomes blocked. This incredible Source of miraculous energy and wisdom available to all of us is unfortunately shielded from us by our own attempts to survive. Our fears, compulsions and preoccupations cause us to ignore *the* most important resource we have, Inner Knowing. In an ironic attempt to gain control over our fears, we block the primary tool available to dissolve them.

Two days after the conversation with my German friends, I traveled about 100 miles southwest to a beautiful area of France along the Moselle River in search of more ancestral roots. While having dinner in a tiny Turkish café one evening and feeling a bit lonely as I missed the joyful camaraderie I had recently enjoyed, I looked out the window to see a *huge* flock of small birds gracefully soaring across the sky. It was an astounding sight! Sitting spellbound for about 20 minutes, I watched the patterns these thousands of birds created as they -- altogether as one large, black dance troupe – dipped, swirled, floated and twirled through the crisp autumn air. I could almost hear classical ballet music accompanying them, as I sank deeper into feeling totally relaxed and serene.

Go into the wilderness and meet yourself.
----- *Enos Mills*

Having just spoken of such phenomenon with my friends, I smiled softly as I recognized the synchronicity of this event. Our conversation had heightened my awareness of how these birds had been beautifully choreographed, waltzing together in perfect patterns, moving in precisely the same direction at the same speed, with flawless timing and absolutely no confusion or disasters. It was fascinating to see small splinter groups join the larger group as they flew in from a distance, spent about 15 seconds integrating themselves into the mass, and then voila! They blended in as part of the whole, and I couldn't distinguish the new dancers from the old. It was a wonderful treat for me, as my feelings of tranquility increased and my loneliness diminished. Just taking a short break out of my day to sit still and receive nature's gift was something I promised myself I would do more often when I returned home to my busy life. Since that day, I am intensely aware of and love watching bird flight patterns. I no longer take them for granted.

One of the most talented songwriters in the 20th century and a man genuinely committed to preserving the environment is the late John Denver. He sings of his love for nature in his song "Sweet Surrender," reminding us how amazing natural gifts can be, especially to teach us about non-resistance. If you take time to carefully listen to his lyrics, hopefully they will continue to play in your mind. "Sweet, sweet surrender. Live, live without care. Like a fish in the water, like a bird in the air."

As many John Denver fans realize, living in the mountains of Colorado can be challenging, as well as exhilarating. As I forged through my fears in Europe, I was grateful to be able to draw upon strength that I had gained through many thrilling Colorado events.

One remarkable method many brave-hearted souls have used to overcome fear is forging through demanding physical experiences in the wilderness. Arriving on the other side of a tough mountaintop challenge can make you feel indomitable.

For me, one such time was a "simple" Outward Bound trek in the snowy, wild forests of Leadville, Colorado, several years prior to my journey. After days of teambuilding and being pushed to our limits, the surprising result for me was that I not only survived each event, but I actually emerged as a group leader! I had no idea I had so much resilience in me, especially regarding physical challenges.

An original life is unexplored territory.
You don't get there by taking a taxi – you
get there by carrying a canoe.

----- *Alan Alda*

One of our assignments was completing a solo trip (with moral support from our partner) through a complex ropes course. As I was wondering when it was finally going to end, swaying slowly across a rope suspension bridge hundreds of feet above roaring rivers, I realized that there was only one direction to go. Forward. Just as with any trial in life. I drew in a deep breath and kept walking.

I had never considered myself especially athletic so these challenges stretched me to my max. In another assignment, we were instructed to aid our blindfolded partners across a metal wire stretched between trees on either side of a feisty mountain river. All this without saying a word and heavy snow pelting our faces. After successfully managing to get my six-foot-three buddy safely to shore, I thought I was home free.

But, alas, another pair was stranded midway on the metal tight-rope, both of them frozen in place by **fear**. Thankfully, something deep within us inspires our human spunk to step up to whatever needs to be done. So I stepped up -- or rather slid up -- but nevertheless managed to assist the two panic-stricken teammates to safety on solid ground. It was clear to me that there was a force greater than myself assisting me every moment of that experience. Whatever physical strength I needed was there, but more importantly the required wisdom, calmness and internal fortitude was also given me.

Because of my willingness to stretch my comfort zone, the delightful outcome of this adventure for me was to feel a delicious increase in my self-worth. I felt strong desire to transfer this newfound confidence to other areas of my life. Witnessing firsthand how fear had immobilized my teammates over the river that day, I could see how fear begins in our minds and then transfers to our

126

physical bodies. *Challenging ourselves to push through fears, risk-taking in new areas that are unfamiliar and allowing ourselves to endure a bit of discomfort as we expand* are all lessons I learned through risking at Outward Bound. When I felt fear along my journey in Europe, I was glad I had those experiences to draw upon. I am still grateful today as I continue to face new challenges on a regular basis.

Letting nature nurture and delight us is a sensory sampling allowing us to use our five senses to their utmost capacity. The more we experience this heightened use and enjoyment of our senses, the more powerful and sensitive they become. Thus, our joy is maximized. And the feeling of being one with nature, of realizing we are actually a part of everything we see, hear, touch, smell and taste, increases our sense of strength and courage. This is such a great high! The ability and desire we have to protect nature's precious gifts thus becomes a natural outpouring of feeling that connection.

Nature is painting for us, day after day, pictures of infinite beauty.

----- *John Ruskin*

Tools for Navigating Through Your Fears

- Take time to be alone and quiet, then write a letter to yourself discussing your dreams, goals and heart's desires. Be sure to include as many emotions as you can, digging deep to identify them. Talk about what you'd like to see happen within the next six months, and also explore long-range goals for the next year or two. Ask a good friend to keep it safe and mail it to you six months from that date. It is interesting to see what your reactions to your statements are down the road.

CHAPTER SEVENTEEN

LOOKING BEYOND APPEARANCES

Two wrongs don't make a right!

. ----- Lois Daish Stewart House,

My wise mother

There is an unconfirmed, but amazing, legend about a poor Scottish farmer whose name was Fleming. One day he heard a cry for help coming from a nearby bog. He dropped his tools and ran to the bog. There, mired to his waist in black muck, was a terrified boy, screaming and struggling to free himself. Farmer Fleming saved the lad from what could have been a slow and terrifying death.

The next day, a fancy carriage pulled up to the Scotsman's sparse surroundings. A nobleman stepped out and introduced himself as the father of the boy Fleming had saved. "I want to repay you," said the nobleman. "You saved my son's life."

"No, I can't accept payment for what I did," the Scottish farmer replied. At that moment, the farmer's own son came to the door.

"Is that your son?" the nobleman asked.

"Yes," the farmer replied proudly.

"I'll make you a deal. Let me provide him with the level of

education my own son will enjoy. If the lad is anything like his father, he'll no doubt grow to be a man we both will be proud of." And that he did.

Farmer Fleming's son attended the very best schools and in time, graduated from St. Mary's Hospital Medical School in London, and went on to become known throughout the world as the noted Sir Alexander Fleming, the discoverer of Penicillin. Years afterward, the same nobleman's son who was saved from the bog was stricken with pneumonia. What saved his life this time? Penicillin.

The name of the nobleman? Lord Randolph Churchill. His son's name?

Sir Winston Churchill.

The moral of the story? Giving is receiving and receiving is giving. This tale also reminds us that we may never realize the impact that each and every one of our actions has upon others.

Part of the sadness I see in the world today is a strong sense of "them against us." Since September, 2001, this sense of separation has become an even wider gap, a *gigantic chasm of fear*. Fear that runs that deep divides people and ultimately damages everyone involved. As the old saying goes, "Anger does more harm to the vessel in which it is stored than to the object onto which it is poured." We can easily translate the word anger to fear, as they are frequently two sides of the same coin. As each of us looks at our own attitudes, reactions and feelings about the troubled state of the world today, it is essential that we examine our own fears.

Commencing to heal our distressed planet begins with each of us individually.

We ask ourselves, who am I to be brilliant, gorgeous, talented, fabulous? ...who are you NOT to be? You are a child of God. Your playing small does not serve the world. There is nothing enlightened about shrinking so that other people won't feel insecure around you. (You) were born to make manifest the glory of God that is within (you).

----- *Marianne Williamson*

As my travels in Europe progressed, I realized more clearly how my meeting people one on one seemed to dissolve my prejudices and increase my respect for all. Even those who had previously seemed strange or scary to me began to appear non-threatening. I began wishing that all people throughout the world could get to know each other individually. I have worked with many clients who, outside my office in their everyday lives, probably appeared frightening or offensive to many. However, as I got to know each of these people personally and as they shared their stories with me, trust grew between us and I could see the hurt child as well as the frightened adult within them. We no longer threatened each other. Our fears subsided. We are all more alike than different, all of us more frightened of the unknown than the known.

Desmond Tutu in his book, *God Has a Dream*, tells us that "God's love is too great to be confined to any one side of a conflict or to any one religion, and our prejudices....are absolutely and utterly ridiculous in God's eyes." He is reminding us that God loves all of us equally and unconditionally and perhaps we should all strive for the same.

As fear increases individually, as well as on a global scale, we can begin to heal ourselves and others by looking at the idea that giving and receiving are one. If more of us were open to dropping our preconceived opinions, our judgments, and instead began offering more unconditional love, we could then accept the miracle-working power in those gifts. That powerful energy impacts both the giver and the receiver. Practicing tolerance toward others ironically helps us *gain* freedom from our *own* quagmire of fears. I find that many people sadly believe just the opposite.

Throughout my journey, I discovered this process as it unfolded right before my eyes. As certain as I am that this exchange of energy does happen, I wasn't conscious of it while it was occurring in the moment. It only became apparent after I had time to process the events. Once I did, insights into the gifts I'd been receiving as I was giving (and giving as I was receiving) were truly amazing! It

132

enabled me to see past dissimilarity into the heart of a person. It helped me reduce my fears.

Life is either a daring
adventure, or nothing.
----- *Helen Keller*

Last year, my daughter and I had the privilege of participating in a weekend affair in Boulder, Colorado, with about 50 teenage exchange students from nine countries in the Middle East. Each student had traveled from their American home, where they were staying for the school year, to meet each other and participate with our Congressional Representative and caring local citizens in a panel discussion. It was so inspiring to hear these students speak honestly from their hearts. They talked about how their preconceived ideas of Americans had dissipated as they had gotten to know us as individual human beings and families. They all agreed they would go home and promote peace between our countries by attempting to present their new view of Americans to their families and friends.

We also spent several hours with the students playing team-building games, and it was a fantastic experience for my daughter and me to get to know these young people as caring, fun and typical teenagers. They were just like American teens. We came away from the experience wondering what the world would be like if more people

133

could experience just one day like this. The fear we have of others who appear "different" from us would melt away as we realize that there are many more similarities than differences. The large majority of people on this planet want to live happily and at peace, loving their family and friends. As I look at all the actions and reactions in the world today, I frequently recall my mother's wise words, "Two wrongs don't make a right."

> *(If) there were none who were discon-*
> *tented with what they have, the world*
> *would never reach for anything better.*
>
> ----- *Florence Nightingale*

Something else I've learned from my clients that was also reinforced for me in Europe is to allow others to give to me while being a happy receiver. We often feel false pride and think we need to be strong, stoic and independent in order to look successful. Or to maintain the façade that masks our fears. Because of that belief, we sometimes deny others the joy of giving. Perhaps it makes us feel vulnerable. We've been taught to be cautious. I sat up straight and squirmed a bit when I read this quote by Anais Nin: "Is devotion to others a cover for the hungers and the needs of the self, of which one is ashamed? I was always ashamed to take. So I gave. It was not a virtue. It was a disguise." It's important to consider intangible gifts as well. For many, love is the most frightening gift to receive, even though most would also quickly respond that it is ultimately the most important.

When practicing the giving/receiving principle, it is easy to trip over one common obstacle...the strings attached to giving and receiving. We frequently give thinking it is really for the other fellow, when the giving is in reality done because we are fulfilling some need *we* have. It is important to check in with ourselves occasionally to identify our motives, as these misperceptions are usually unconscious. Even subtle manipulation harms all involved. Conditional giving creates mistrust and fear, as power and control issues hide beneath the act of giving.

The corrosive effects of avoidance also exact their toll on our emotional lives. Consistently choosing safety over adventure, brakes over accelerator, no over yes, and consistently preferring to be a passive observer rather than an active participant in our own lives can readily bring on anger and remorse, sorrow and frustration.

----- *Gregg Levoy*

Tools for Navigating Through Your Fears

- Write your first response to reading about the giving/receiving principle. What specific situations in your life did you recall as you were contemplating this chapter? Ask yourself these questions:
    - Have I ever been unwilling to receive or to ask for something I need?
    - Do I ever give with conditions or expectations attached to my gift?
    - How do I feel when I allow others to give to me?
    - How do I feel as I freely give unconditionally?
    - Do you think that giving and receiving are essential to our own well-being?

LET GO AND LET GOD......

AS CHILDREN BRING THEIR
BROKEN TOYS, WITH TEARS
FOR US TO MEND, I BROUGHT
MY BROKEN DREAMS TO GOD,
BECAUSE HE WAS MY FRIEND.
BUT THEN, INSTEAD OF LEAVING
HIM IN PEACE TO WORK ALONE,
I HUNG AROUND AND TRIED TO
HELP, WITH WAYS THAT WERE
MY OWN. AT LAST I SNATCHED
THEM BACK AND CRIED, "HOW
CAN YOU BE SO SLOW?" "MY
CHILD," HE SAID, "WHAT COULD I
DO? YOU NEVER DID LET GO."

- After re-reading Gregg Levoy's statement about "the corrosive effects of avoidance," write a paragraph or two describing one way that you have (in the past or present) chosen safety over adventure, brakes over accelerator, no over yes, or have become a passive observer rather than an active participant. (i.e. you express concern about environmental issues on the planet, but you don't become involved in any activity to actually do anything about the problems)

CHAPTER EIGHTEEN

ALL PEOPLE SMILE IN THE SAME LANGUAGE

Open a new window, open a new door,
travel a new highway that's never been
tried before.
You find you're a dull fellow, punching
the same clock, walking the same tightrope
as everyone on the block.

The fellow you ought to be is three dimen-
sional, soaking up life down to your toes.
Whenever they say you're slightly unconven-
tional, just put your thumb up to your nose....
And show them how to...dance to a new
rhythm, whistle a new love song, toast to
a new vintage, the fizz doesn't fizz too long!
There's only one way to make the bubbles stay.

---- Jerry Herman
From "Open a New Window"
The Musical "Mame"

While in Europe I had many opportunities to practice receiving. At times mere acquaintances offered me a warm bed, food or companionship. Despite our language differences, many other kind people I didn't even know responded very patiently to my confusion and questions. The theme of my trip became: *All People Smile In the Same Language!* A warm smile, eye contact, a little effort to be courteous and genuine attempts to speak their language (rather than automatically expecting them to speak mine) worked wonders.

In the 1970's, a very sensitive physician named Dr. Jerald Jampolsky, after visiting with a young boy who was dying, realized that patients need to be treated in a more holistic manner. The concept of healing the entire being, not just the body, merged into his dedication to improve the medical community's methods, and he began the international movement now called Attitudinal Healing (AH). These principles include believing that healing is inner peace and letting go of fear and that love is the most important healing force in the world.

Having attended the AH International Conference and training to facilitate their groups, two important ideas I learned became very helpful to me throughout my journey:

❖ We can always perceive ourselves and others as either extending love or giving a call for help.
❖ We can become love-finders rather than fault-finders.

It's absolutely astonishing to try these out and watch the results! They are ultimately able to melt away defensiveness and attack, two critically important issues linked to fear. When I encountered individuals on my path that I perceived as rude or uncooperative, I tried to see them as giving a call for help or love, rather than taking it personally and letting it ruin my moment or day. That's not always an easy thing to do. If I found myself becoming critical of others, I attempted to be a love-finder instead. As I did that, I realized that if I was becoming judgmental it was often because I was tired, fearful or in a negative mental state myself. It had nothing to do with anyone else. These are difficult beliefs to accept and put into practice, even with our loved ones, but well worth the effort.

To aspire for something more than the daily grind is a great and noble thing. But to go out in the world and achieve it is to have the sky under your hands.

----- *John F. Kennedy*

The French use the word "apprendre" as a verb that means *both* "to teach" and "to learn," which in itself teaches us much. This ties into the theory that not only are giving and receiving the same, but that we are all students and all teachers to each other as well. If we can lighten up, relax and begin to view every instant of each day as an opportunity to learn, then we will be more open to receiving in every moment as well. Even those moments that try our patience. Events that initially appear to be frightening often dissolve as we develop these attitudes. Many times our greatest teachers throughout life are those people or circumstances that are either the most loving or the most difficult in our lives.

Our vision of what is happening is up to us.

Another piece to being open to receiving and learning is the premise that when the student is ready, the teacher will appear. I began to see this on a regular basis. Teachers and students meet when they are ready to meet. It's as though our paths run parallel for a period of time and then, almost magically, at the perfect moment, the paths intersect. The great part is that we don't have to strive or struggle to know how, when or where those lives will touch. We *need only be open.* Open to any and all experiences, closed to and prejudiced about nothing.

Thinking that we know what we *must* have keeps us from recognizing pleasures in an unexpected moment.

I have often found it challenging to balance wanting --- having dreams, expectations and desires --- with accepting, or going with the flow. My journey helped me learn to chill out and allow my Spiritual Radar System to guide me to my good, without abandoning my goals. If we each look back on the gifts life has given us, many have arrived in the form of unanticipated opportunities. Being open, flexible and spontaneous allows for those unexpected events or people to play their role in our expansion and growth. And, teachers don't always come gift wrapped in pretty paper but are often disguised as "problems." I could fill many pages telling about all the teachers I had on my journey, but I would like to share a few. They seemed to arrive with impeccable timing. Looking back, almost all turned into giving/ receiving scenarios. I often thought I was doing all the receiving at the time, but I now realize that I had been giving as well. We all benefited!

Fear is the lock, laughter the key
to your heart.

----- *Stephen Stills,*
From "Suite, Judy Blue Eyes"

The most obvious moment of meeting someone "by chance" was bumping into a friendly Australian mate who gave me the gift of helping me find my playfulness and spunk again. Only after we parted did I realize the importance of our meeting.

I had been in the south of France for a few days and was walking along the beach roadside when I overheard an American woman talking to a small group of men. I had no idea what the circumstances were, but since it had been days since I had spoken English with anyone and was craving in-depth communication, I decided to boldly nudge into their conversation. Joyce was a very gregarious gal from Austin, Texas, who was in France on business and had joined some Australians who were also there for their business. The group invited me to go to Monte Carlo for the day, so we headed out to find the bus station. That's when the fun began. We all enjoyed the exchange of stories from home and comparing cultures, as well as sharing beautiful sights, laughter galore and delicious Mediterranean food and wine.

One of the most fun-loving Australian blokes was a sensitive engineer/rugby player, Buzz, with whom I spent time throughout the next week. It began to dawn on me that we were each giving and receiving some things of value that we needed at that moment, mostly the ability to share safely and intimately about our dreams, fears, values and loves. I felt as though a guardian angel had put me in the right place at the right time, and him as well. We touched each other's lives in special ways, getting to know each other deeply in ways that normally would take months. Why? I'm not completely sure, but I do know that we were both giving and receiving unconditional acceptance for that time. We were living out the AH principle of no fault-finding, and that always feels wonderful! We were also teaching and learning at the same time. As he rode off to the airport the day we parted, he blew me a kiss from his taxi window. I felt gratitude for our chance meeting. I know he did as well.

To cheat oneself out of love is the most terrible deception. It is an eternal loss for which there is no reparation, neither in time nor in eternity.

-----*Soren Kierkegaarde*

Tools for Navigating Through Your Fears

- Name one event in your life you initially labeled a "problem" but later you viewed it as a blessing and became thankful for it having been in your life.

- Think of a time when someone (a co-worker, family member or stranger) pushed your anger button and all you could feel was annoyance. Try to imagine that they were actually filled with fear and were giving a cry for help. Does this help you at all in becoming a love-finder rather than a fault-finder? The next step in this process is to catch yourself the *next* time you feel attacked by someone and stop to consider that they may be calling for love. You have a choice about an alternative reaction. (Please note: this is not a recommendation that you become passive and tolerate any type of emotional or verbal abuse – it is simply an exercise in perception-switch when you are feeling annoyed!)

CHAPTER NINETEEN

ANGELS DISGUISED AS FRIENDS

*There is enough in the world for every-
one to have plenty to live on happily
and to be at peace with his neighbors.*

      ----- *Harry S. Truman*

One of the most generous and loving "angels" that took me under her wings in France was an American college friend. Barb had moved to Paris shortly after college and married a Frenchman. I had had *no* contact with her for over 25 years, but when I "happened" to bump into a mutual friend on my way out of the country, she suggested I contact our French connection via email. Barb wrote back and invited me to stay for a few days at her home two hours south of Paris.

We both felt a bit awkward upon meeting again after so long, but it didn't take long before we both felt like we'd known each other closely all these years. Her nature is pure, honest love. She shared her home, food and family with me, and I relaxed and had an absolutely fantastic time! Throughout our time together, I also felt like she was receiving something from me that she needed in that

146

moment, whether it was to connect to another American woman, speak English again, talk about matters of the heart, discuss children and men, or simply sit and have tea and laugh heartily over silly nothings.

One of the greatest gifts Barb gave me was in the magnificent cathedral where she gives tours in French and English. She teaches hundreds of visitors not only about St. Etienne's mystical secrets, but she also enlightens with her lessons of depth, meaning and value through stories of people long ago. After we entered this glorious structure, she pulled up two chairs and sat me down. Then, in detail, she explained the Prodigal Son narrative created upon one of the many two-story, extraordinary stained glass windows in this huge, ancient church. I was *mesmerized*. Her love for the cathedral and her work oozed as enthusiasm from her, and I was reminded of how important it is to love what we do as we busily go about making a living.

You must be the change you
wish to see in the world.
----- Mahatma Gandhi

At her home I watched her exhaust herself through her devotion to meeting the many and varied needs of her four children. I could see myself and many other women as well who had forgotten how to stop and make time for themselves. I believe a gift I gave her in return for her kindness was a reminder that she deserved and needed to nurture herself occasionally, not just her family. Our story is still not complete, as I know I have more in return to offer her and her family some day, but I also know that in her giving, and through my *allowing* her to do so, valuable lessons for both of us were learned.

Sometimes receiving is actually giving someone the gift of being able to give. It is important for all of us to understand how natural and wise it is to ask for help when we need it. It is also wonderful to allow others to share with us what they have to give. As givers, our "reciprocated favors" don't always come back to us directly from the person to whom we gave. It is again part of the theory that we are all one, and when we give love we receive love. How, when or from whom we are given love in return is a surprise we can anticipate receiving, perhaps when we least expect it!

Our cultural training reinforces toughness, independence and self-sufficiency, so the idea of asking for what we need is indeed difficult. What is often called for is *strength enough to be soft*, and yes, even vulnerable. Ironically, that actually works to *lessen* fear within us. Experiment with dropping your tough façade and allowing yourself to be a bit more vulnerable in a specific situation, and see if your fear isn't reduced. It's a form of risk-taking that increases courage and self esteem, while diminishing anxiety.

148

The trail is the thing, not the end
of the trail. Travel too fast, and
you miss all you are traveling for.

----- *Louis L'Amour*

Throughout my journey I began to heighten my awareness of incoming miracles. I have continually endeavored to achieve this same level of attentiveness since my return home. The key is to actually **stop** striving and instead to relax. In an easy-going, non-resistive state, I am better able to enjoy each and every moment. When I'm caught up in my fast-paced, daily routine, it is more of a challenge to tune into each beautiful moment, every spectacular encounter with another human being or even the gifts of nature. These next stories helped me, however, to fine-tune these skills.

Another angel who gifted me with more life lessons was Karin, one of the happiest, most authentic people I've ever known. Traveling from her small hometown in Germany a few years ago to attend a workshop in California was a challenge she loved. And that is where we met. We corresponded for two years before she invited me to "stop by" while on my journey. She, her husband Helmut and their three delightful teenage children became instant family to me. They *live* unconditional love. We connected in Koln, Germany, at the austere Koln Cathedral next to the train station. I recognized Karin immediately with her warm smile and matching dimples. Our adventures began in the cathedral where we spent an hour viewing a spectacular exhibit of Rubens' artwork. The fun and learning

149

continued throughout the five days I spent in their small, friendly village.

As tired as I was the evening I arrived, (I had proudly and successfully manipulated my way through the Paris Metro and various trains along the route) Karin whisked me off to her hometown to sit in a quaint, serene church to listen to her choir rehearse. What a contrast to my hectic travel day! The choir was practicing songs for their Christmas program, and it was a delightful treat. I felt as though I'd been transported that day via TGV (the speedy trains in France) to Heaven, and I was being serenaded by THE choir. I requested that they sing "Stille Nacht," which of course is our American favorite "Silent Night," and they happily agreed. I had goose bumps as I soaked up those angel voices. This was just the first hour of my stay in rural Germany.

The hush of heaven holds my heart today.
How quietly do all things fall in place....
this is the day that I finally learn that there
is no need that I do anything. In Him has
every choice already been made. In Him has
every conflict been resolved. In Him is every-
thing I hope to find already been given."
      ----- *"A Course in Miracles," Lesson # 286*

Tools for Navigating Through Your Fears

- Think about your relationships for a moment and ask yourself if they are reciprocal. Is there giving and receiving exchanged?

- And in those relationships where you do more of the giving, (let's say you are a caretaker for someone) how do you feel as you're giving?

- Finally, check your feelings (especially your gut-level emotions) when thinking of a relationship where you feel like someone else is doing more of the giving, with you giving the gift of receiving. Are you able to let this person give as you graciously receive?

CHAPTER TWENTY

GIVING THE GIFT OF RECEIVING

*The most important thing is to realize
why one is alive - and I think it is not
only to build bridges or tall buildings or
make money, but to do something truly
important, to do something for humanity.
To bring joy, hope, to make life richer for
the spirit because you have been alive,
that is the most important thing.*

----- *Artur Rubinstein*

I had no idea the gifts in store for me the following days as I followed Karin and Helmut through their daily routines. They wanted me to experience "normal German life," but it seemed anything but hum-drum to me. I chuckled watching "The Simpsons" speak German on their T.V. and was intrigued by their take on American politics. Did I mention how fantastic the German bread and wine is? I suddenly realized why my family had always been so excited about spending Thanksgiving Day with my dear German aunt who loved to cook!

One day Karin took me to work with her to an assisted living residence for people who are developmentally disabled. That day turned into an unexpected surprise. Her job is distributing money for the government to various agencies that support and treat people in need, and it sounded fairly routine to me. While Karin attended a meeting, a kind lady escorted me to a large complex where mentally handicapped persons complete their specific daily jobs. Some painted dishes or boxed up kitchen utensils, depending on their level of skill. That was the day that I truly learned that all people smile in the same language! They were speaking **Joy,** the universal language, and so was I. The fact that I knew very little German made no difference in the way we connected. They were pure, genuine, happy folks who didn't care where I was from, if I could speak or not, what I looked like or how influential or prestigious I was.

They were all about love.

They proudly showed me their tasks and accomplishments and politely escorted me through the various workplaces. As one man saw us approaching, he slyly pulled out his comb to style the three hairs on his head and smiled shyly as he showed us his work. He glowed with pride and happiness. I was impressed with how concerned the Germans are that their people in need feel productive and have a sense of accomplishment. Karin explained that money is not the issue. They believe in making sure *all* their citizens are taken care of.

154

Participating in the celebration of life in-
volves taking risks, so I go for it all the time.
----- *Susan Smith Jones, Ph.D.*

As we talked on our long drive back home that evening, Karin shared her viewpoint of the struggles East Germans have had as their "wall of familiarity" came tumbling down in 1989. After spending more than 40 years behind this wall, much of the East German's attitude reflected the single desire to have what others on the "other side" were experiencing. To be able to live where the grass seemed greener, so to speak. Because they weren't allowed to have free enterprise, they weren't competitive. So, instead of rivaling each other or spending day after day concerned with making money, they bonded together supporting each other against their common enemy, the Communists.

When freedom was finally gained, they actually lost valuable, non-tangible gifts they had taken for granted. The East Germans had spent many hours of many days and into years wishing their lives could be different. They often failed to simply enjoy the moment at hand. The ties of love and unity that were created out of this situation had often gone unnoticed. I had the impression that because their focus was on the bananas they wanted so badly, but couldn't have, this focus kept them from appreciating the assets at hand. Their new-found freedom has caused problems, as they have lost a life that was very comfortable, perhaps easier. So it goes with us all. The

155

more freedom we have, the less secure we feel and the more responsibility we have to assume. Their trials can serve as an important reminder to all of us to examine the positives and negatives in a situation, as we don't always recognize the wonderful "fruit" in our own back yards.

One of the highlights of my entire journey throughout Europe was in another small rural German village I visited the morning I left my friends to return to France. I had just spent several days with the two friends of Karin & Helmut I mentioned earlier. They are two very authentic and genuinely loving men, as well as incredibly talented musicians. Thomas and Karl gave me (in addition to their laughter, tenderness and passion for life) a most beautiful gift at 7:00 a.m. on my last morning in Germany.

The antidote to exhaustion is wholeheartedness.

-----Brother David Steindl-Rast

They invited me, along with Karin and Helmut, to a 900 year-old humble, stone church for a musically-inspired meditation. We entered the church out of complete darkness and saw a single candle burning in the entryway. We carefully made our way in, each to our own invisible pews, and sat in darkness as the angelic music began to fill the ancient chapel. Just as the stone building had magically appeared out of the morning fog, the melodic tenor and bass voices

156

came out of the dark and softly surrounded us. I felt the spirits of all the people who had worshipped in that sanctuary for nearly one thousand years wrapping me in peace. Soon the sound of a sweet violin joined the voices, as did a rich grand piano. Their tranquility enveloped me completely.

I savored the moment.

Eventually, I began to see sunlight gently spreading color and form on a single, small stained-glass window behind the altar. As the earth turned further, I began to notice the many symbols this Christian church incorporated into its simple décor. The last pastor, who had served many years, designated this church as a place for universal worship. He had invited other religious beliefs and symbols into the sanctuary, as well as into the hearts of the worshippers. Again, it was a reminder to me of our oneness with all, everywhere and always present.

The music became a bridge between my human self and my Higher Self, as I experienced incredible contentment and peace. I had a *knowing* that there was nothing for me to fear. What a beautiful way to feel, to *be*, and with absolute assuredness. I wanted to hold on to that hour, that peace, forever. I know I can, if I so choose. I have to consciously take myself back to that state, however. It certainly doesn't happen automatically. In fact, as I was making my way through the Koln train station later that afternoon and feeling nervous about details and how to's, I realized that even so soon after this wonderful experience I was again feeling fear about absolute petty nothingness. I knew then that to retain that peace would indeed be a challenge.

The good news is that I quickly recognized the loss of the serenity, distinctly felt fear replace love and knew I had the ability to return to a calm state. It worked like a charm! I felt very empowered, knowing that I always have Universal Energy within me and available in every instant. Being able to change my entire outlook in a few moments felt fantastic, and I felt fear fleeing from my heart. I often recall those precious "angels" serenading me when I need to return to a peaceful state.

God is the pen writing a love
letter to humanity through you.
----- *Rev. Christopher Chenoweth*

Tools for Navigating Through Your Fears

- Can you think of ways you allow art, music or other forms of creative expression to nurture, enliven and/or de-stress you? How can you increase these gifts in your life and heighten your awareness of them as healing instruments?

- As you recall the story my friend Karin told me about the East Germans being unhappy by focusing on what was missing, contemplate and explore your heart by asking it: "Are there any situations in my life that arouse envy or that I complain about because I think not having some "thing" is keeping my happiness from me?

- This is a good time to stop and make a Grateful List. Having an attitude of gratitude is the best antidote for self-pity and depression. Reviewing your list daily, as well as adding new items regularly, is a life-long investment that works wonders.

CHAPTER TWENTY-ONE

SURRENDER TO LIVE

When I find myself in times of trouble,
mother Mary comes to me, speaking words
of wisdom, Let it Be.... And when the night
is cloudy there is still a light that shines on
me....There will be an answer, Let it Be.

----- *Paul McCartney*
From "Let It Be"

When my daughter was in eighth grade, I made her a Tinker-bell outfit for her for Halloween parties, complete with a blue, sparkly magic wand. I enchantingly created this wand from antique sequins my grandmother had when she was young. Somehow, my grand-mother's love seemed to enliven this wand and make it magical indeed. Since that Halloween I have kept the wand in my counseling office, showing it to clients early in our talks. It symbolizes my conviction that, although I may not have magical answers for them, I do believe they have within them all the answers they need. My task is simply to love them while encouraging them to love themselves, believe in their unused potential, direct them in being gentle with themselves and others and assist them in the courageous undertaking of finding their true Self buried beneath the superficial details of daily life.

Do you really want to know the magical answer for overcoming all those pesky fears and worries you have? (Drum roll while I wave my blue magic wand!)

The answer is in one simple word.

Surrender.

Simple. But not easy. I once conducted a survey asking, "What are the most important issues you would like to work on in your life?" The number one response was "Letting Go."

> *I rid myself of my doubts by*
> *remembering there is a valid*
> *reason for everything that happens.*
> ----- Dr. Wayne Dyer

Most of us realize we fret and worry too much, but we truly don't know how to eliminate the continual, subtle fear that hovers around us like an innocent grey cloud. I've already talked about how we must face our fears, rather than continue to avoid them, because as long as we're alive new will fears pop up. And we cannot change behaviors unless we admit they are there. As we own up to, then gently accept our fears, (without beating up on ourselves for having them) that honesty with self then assists us in our resolve to eradicate the fear.

Eradicating fear is an extremely difficult request for most of us, *unless we have a belief in some Divine Power to help us in our determination to change.* This is the beauty of surrender. We need to be able to toss away the fiery ball of fear and know that a Power stronger and wiser than we are will catch it and dissolve it into nothingness. What's even better is when you finally realize that Power is *within you!* Working in the field of addictions, I have had much exposure to the remarkable Alcoholics Anonymous (AA) Program. The simple philosophy of AA teaches what wise sages over the centuries have been saying: Amazing miracles can and do occur if we are willing to accept and practice a few treasured principles. First, admit we've often made a mess of our lives and that we truly don't have control over anything outside of ourselves. Next, open ourselves to the idea that there might be a Power that is more knowing than we are. Then, as we are willing to let go, relax and allow this Power to take over, our lives can be transformed.

*Settle yourself in solitude, and you
will come upon God in yourself.*

----- *Teresa of Avila*

162

Addicts begin their journey into recovery by admitting their powerlessness over substances, but this process can certainly be applied to any area of your life, including excessive worrying. So, the kick-off begins by you admitting you have problems with fear and acknowledging that you are powerless over most of the circumstances that aggravate your anxieties. I do realize this is going to initially cause *more* fear, but please don't give up quite yet. Remember that the only way to feel in control is to admit that we actually have none. Letting go of trying to control is truly the method for regaining a sense of control. This phenomenon of control is similar to a Chinese finger puzzle --- the harder you try to pull it apart, the tighter it becomes.

My friends in addiction recovery call this process "surrendering to live." It doesn't mean giving up on yourself, but rather *giving up the outcome* of any situation to the Divine Intelligence that knows best. It doesn't mean becoming a doormat, and it doesn't mean giving up your goals or dreams. It is the first step you take toward the solution as you walk away from the problem. It is allowing your body, mind and soul to relax and become calm enough to hear possible alternatives to what you've been experiencing. Surrender enables you to let the Energy that is within you flow freely through you, as you. It's about allowing.

If I had not been practicing these principles for years prior to my journey, I question whether I would have even taken the risk to give up what I had to in order to make this trip. To trust that my inner knowing was leading me in the right direction. I'm not certain I would have had the courage to leap into the unknown, building my wings on the way down. I faced each challenge, one at a time, drawing on my belief that surrendering to live truly works. My fear was reduced or eliminated as I genuinely released outcomes and practiced non-resistance. It's such an irony, such a contrast to what we're generally taught!

The spiritual journey is one of continually falling on your face, getting up, brushing yourself off, looking sheepishly at God, and taking another step.

----- *Aurobindo*

One of the positive aspects of life today is the trend of allowing people to experiment with their own vision, their own view of their Higher Power. I firmly believe each of us needs to define that Power individually, as it fits within our own convictions. Through teachings of my mother, grandmother and many other mentors, I have formed a belief that the Source of *my* being is not an old, white-haired man sitting on a throne up in heaven. However, this may be *your* picture of your Higher Power. Whatever works for you should be gratefully embraced.

I see all of us as extensions of Divine Love. For me this God-force is All-Powerful and All-Knowing, so it stands to reason that we have this Power and Wisdom within us as well. Spirit is simply the deeper dimension of our human selves. If you are sincere in wanting to change the way fear controls your life, I encourage you to explore what really makes *your* heart tick.

And to start you on that exploration, there are two thoughts that might be helpful for you to consider. The first is a question: "*Would you rather be right or happy?*" The second I suggest you put in large letters on your bathroom mirror and act as if it is true for one month:

"*I have resigned as General Manager of the Universe.*"

Resigning as General Manager means you *get* to let go of needing to have all the answers, for everything and everyone all the time. Including your own. You get to take a sabbatical and start relaxing. Watch what happens. Perhaps the magic wand within you is beginning to glisten!

There are only two ways to live your life. One is as though nothing is a miracle. The other is as if everything is.

----- *Albert Einstein*

Tools for Navigating Through Your Fears

- When you hear my suggestion to "surrender to live," what is your first, heartfelt reaction? What emotions and thoughts does it stir within you? Write about not only your feelings, but explain what surrender means to you. How can you make it a powerful, positive force in your life?

- What is your picture of your Higher Power? (If you've never explored this, be gentle with yourself and proceed slowly – simply begin to experiment with the idea that there may be a Loving Intelligence that shares its Strength with you.)

- Using a full sheet of paper, write a letter to your Higher Power and just chat like you were writing your best friend. Express what is in your heart.

- Answer this question and discuss on paper why you chose the answer you did: *Would you rather be right or happy?* (Choose only ONE, right *or* happy!)

- Make yourself a nice little banner to be placed above your bathroom mirror (or anywhere else you choose where you'll see it daily) with these words: "I have resigned as General Manager of the Universe." After one week of soaking that in, write a page about your reactions to it, positive and negative, and what you've learned about yourself because of it.

CHAPTER TWENTY-TWO

DON'T JUST DO SOMETHING, SIT THERE

*Tend to your vital heart, and all
you worry about will be solved.*

----- *Rumi*

Just for one moment, imagine releasing all of your cares and arriving at a point of peace without an ounce of worry about the next hour, day, week or year. What if God really is in charge of *everything*? Practicing the Presence or making conscious contact with the Divine within you changes YOU, not God. As you become calm and get your human self out of the way, you allow this Love to merge with and flow through you. Answers you have been looking for, especially peace of mind, have their opportunity to be released. It's called letting God be God.

One word that became very meaningful to me along my journey is *non-resistance*. I see misery abound (in myself and others) when we waste our energy "pushing against" whatever we perceive is the block of the day. The beauty of surrender is that we become non-resistive. Much like my Outward Bound experience, this requires trust in the Divine within us as we practice flowing, easily and gently, with those situations and people that we like, *as well as those we don't*. Once we are in an unruffled state, when we decide to take action, it is more likely to be productive and appropriate.

My Unity minister and wonderful mentor in Colorado, Jack Groverland, says it well. "Faith is having faith in circumstances when they seem to be blessing your personal desires, or even when they don't seem to be going with your personal desire." There is serenity to be found, as Jack reminds us, "in accepting each event as being there by Divine Appointment." Eventually, if we can learn to "have our only affirmation in life be 'This also is of God,' we will be truly enlightened." Perhaps blissful, as well. Along my route in Europe, seeing how much happier I was when practicing non-resistance, I witnessed peace and joy in myself time after time.

Only those who see the invisible
can do the impossible.

----- *Author Unknown*

The medical profession has proven that when we are stressed and tense our energy is restricted, our blood pressure increases and our immune system is weakened, just to mention a few consequences. You can probably feel the difference in your body when you are happy versus fearful, such as experiencing an upset stomach, neck and back pain or headaches.

169

This same concept holds true for Divine Energy. *It cannot do its job if we're not allowing*, if we're restricting or blocking off its flow. Probably the first step in learning to let go is to mentally stop beating up on yourself. Rather than trying to tune into God with fists clinched, jaw tight and muscles tense, why not begin by telling yourself what a fantastic creation you are? Take a moment to appreciate how marvelous you are. You don't have to believe it 100%, just acknowledge the wonder in yourself. Next, stop the "monkeys in your head" from chattering on and on about your concerns and worries. Catch your thoughts and then most tenderly bid them adieu, without an ounce of criticism toward yourself for having them. As I have said, I imagine myself dumping my perceived troubles into a sparkling mountain stream and as they flow downstream, I smile and remind myself that I've released them. I often have to repeat this process more than once!

Now, ask yourself in this specific moment if you are holding on to any regrets, resentments or resistance from which you want to be free. Or, if you are focused on the past or future, try to bring your mind and heart back to the present moment. Again, let resistance to any of this simply float away. Then, become still and just dissolve into Divine Love.

Learn to listen with your heart.

But the truth of the matter is that each
one of us is meant to have that space
inside where we can hear God's voice.
God is available to all of us. God says,
'Be still and know that I am God.'
                    -----Archbishop Desmond Tutu,
                    1984 Nobel Peace Prize recipient

Meditation and relaxation techniques are many and varied these days, and there are an abundance of resources available to teach you how to use these valuable tools. Experiment until you find the method that works best for you. Keep in mind that you shouldn't get hung up on the technique, but rather just learn to be still. You can't do it wrong if it feels right for you. Part of my ability to surrender and tune into my Source during my journey was my *devotion* to taking time to be still. It was my priority.

Again, one of my primary methods for going within is to be out in nature. Music is also one of my favorites, whether I am dancing up a storm to rock, or quietly listening to a single flute. Painting a picture, skydiving, doing tai chi, petting a purring cat, kneading bread, rafting down a serene river, watching a movie or play, taking a walk or holding a sleeping infant are other ways that I know people use to relax and open themselves to the Divine Flow. The point is to raise your consciousness to a level that takes you beyond the activity to what is greater within you.

When I am disconnected from Spirit, I feel it in the depth of my being. I describe it as being out of balance, just as my car reacts when the tires are out of balance. There is a shaking in my "steering mechanism" that is as obvious as my auto's reminder to me that something needs adjusting. The old expression goes "When you don't feel close to God, ask yourself 'Who moved?'" A quote I read years ago helps me re-center myself when I'm internally bouncing around:

"In letting go concern, I open the way for an inrush of God's transforming power. As I let God take over, I am filled with feelings of peace and freedom. I am able to go about my life with a calm and confident spirit, sure of God's presence, sure of right out-workings in all my affairs."

I've said this to myself for decades, and it continues to bring me peace as I remind myself to lighten up.

It is not you who shape God;
it is God that shapes you.
If then you are the work of God,
Await the hand of the Artist who
does all things in due season.
Offer the Potter your heart, soft
and tractable,
And keep the form in which the

Artist has fashioned you.
Let your clay be moist,
Lest you grow hard and lose the
imprint of the Potter's fingerprints."

----- *Author Unknown*

Just days before I returned home from my journey, I stood on that hillside next to the "Retrouver Statue" at the Bascilica in Lourdes, France, and gently gazed down upon hundreds of candles lit by people with enormous faith. I felt deep appreciation for every ray of brilliant light beaming from each candle. The tranquility I felt was paradoxically mixed with an incredible feeling of invincibility and strength. I was completely peaceful, as all fear had vanished. I simply knew that all was well.

At that moment I realized all I had gained in just a few short months. I also knew this kind of transformation is possible for anyone and everyone. I felt very excited to go home and share my findings with others. If you so desire and are willing to build your wings along the way, I believe you, too, can change feeling overwhelmed with worry to serenity and peace. As you read this final poem that a dear friend of mine shared with me on my birthday, please hear it as my encouragement to you to begin on *your* journey today. I am holding you in my heart. Blessings to you on your path, my friend!

I am your friend, and my love for you goes deep.

There is nothing I can give you which you have not got.

But there is much, very much, that while I can not give it, you can take.

No heaven can come to us unless our hearts find rest in today. Take Heaven!

No peace lies in the future which is not hidden in this present little instant. Take Peace!

The gloom of the world is but a shadow.

Behind it, yet within our reach, is Joy.

There is radiance and glory in the darkness could we but see,

And to see we have only to look. I beseech you to look.

Life is so generous a giver, but we, judging its gifts by the covering,

Cast them away as ugly, or heavy, or hard.

Remove the covering and you will find beneath it a living splendor, woven of Love, by Wisdom, with Power.

Welcome It, grasp It and you touch the Angel's hand that brings It to you.

Everything that we call a trial, a sorrow, or a duty, believe me, that Angel's hand is there:

The gift is there, and the wonder of an overshadowing Presence.

Our joys too: be not content with them as joys, they too conceal Diviner gifts.

Life is so full of meaning and purpose,
So full of beauty beneath its covering that you will find earth but cloaks your heaven.
Courage then to claim it: that is all!
But courage you have: and the knowledge that we are pilgrims together wending through unknown country, home.

And so, at this time I greet you not quite as the world sends greetings,
But with profound esteem and with the prayer that for you, now and forever,
The day breaks, and the shadows flee away.

--- Written in 1513 AD by Fra Giovanni

Tools for Navigating Through Your Fears

- When I discuss "non-resistance," what is your response? Does the thought of letting go evoke any fear in you? What specific situations/people in your life do you have the most difficulty releasing control over? And what is one example of a situation or person that you seem to be "pushing against" in some form or another, and how do you end up feeling when you know you are doing this?

- In the lovely ancient poem by Fra Giovanni, write about your thoughts and feelings regarding these lines: " Life is so full of meaning and purpose, so full of beauty beneath its covering that you will find earth but cloaks your heaven. Courage then to claim it: that is all! But courage you have...."

- Remember the list of fears you wrote following Chapter 2 and revised later? Get it out and look at it again. Go back over it and (chuckling a bit) see if any of these now seem less overwhelming. Check in with yourself to see if you can look at any of those fears and eliminate them from your list (due to the fact that they don't seem to have the impact on you that you initially believed they did). With any left over, ask yourself how much longer you wish to allow them to have power over your precious life. You are free to dismiss any you want at any time!

SUGGESTED READINGS
FROM THE AUTHOR

Albom, Mitch. *Tuesdays With Morrie: An Old Man, A Young Man, and Life's Greatest Lesson.* Doubleday Publishing, 1997.

Breathnach, Sara Ban. *Something More.* Warner Books, 2000.

Butterworth, Eric. *Discover the Power Within You.* HarperCollins Publishers, 1989.

Clinebell, Howard, Dr. *Ecotherapy: Healing Ourselves, Healing the Earth.* Barnes and Noble Books, 1995.

Dyer, Wayne W., Dr. *The Power of Intention.* Hay House, Inc., 2004.

Freeman, James Dillet and Maday, Michael A., Editor. *Angels Sing in Me: The Best of James Dillet Freeman.* Unity House, 2004.

Gordon, Sol and Brutcher, Harold. *Life is Uncertain, Eat Dessert First!* Delacorte Press, 1990.

Groverland, Jack. *Miracles Made Easy*. Bigtree Press, 1985.

Hawkins, David Dr. *Power Versus Force*. Hay House, Inc., 2002.

Jeffers, Susan, Ph.D. *Feel the Fear and Do It Anyway*. Fawcett Columbine, 1987.

John-Roger and McWilliams, Peter. *Life 101: Everything We Wish We Had Learned About Life in School - But Didn't*. Prelude Press, 1991.

Jones, Susan Smith, Ph.D. *Choose to Be Healthy*. Celestial Arts, 1987.

Levoy, Gregg. *Callings: Finding and Following Your Authentic Life*. Three Rivers Press, 1997.

Reman, Rachel Naomi, M.D. *Kitchen Table Wisdom*. Riverhead Books, 1997

Rosemergy, Jim. *A Closer Walk with God*. Acropolis Books, Inc., 1997.

Shain, Merle. *Hearts That We Broke Long Ago*. Bantam Books, 1983.

Tutu, Desmond. *God Has a Dream: A Vision of Hope for Our Time*. Doubleday Publishers, 2004.

ABOUT THE AUTHOR

Susan Elaine Stewart is an adventurer, writer, photographer and traveler. She began counseling in the addictions field in 1982 at the Harmony Foundation in Estes Park, Colorado, and also worked as a family therapist at the Betty Ford Center in Rancho Mirage, California. She opened a private counseling practice in 1989 in Estes Park, and has been teaching at the University of Colorado in Boulder since 2001. Her sense of adventure, skills as a therapist and deep spiritual convictions have inspired Susan to create numerous articles which have been published over the past 15 years. As a believer in the effectiveness of group interaction/support, as well as in the innate desire of people to fulfill their potential, she is available to facilitate workshops and give presentations. To reach Susan, you may write her at: _SusanStewart@peakviewpublications.com_ or view her website at peakviewpublications.com. Susan loves spending time with her two adult children, Brandon and Jocelyn, and calls Colorado her home base.